W9-AGB-905

BACK TO BATAAN

BACK
·TO·
BATAAN

JEROME CHARYN

FARRAR · STRAUS · GIROUX

New York

Copyright © 1993 by Jerome Charyn

All rights reserved

Originally published in French translation as *Une petite histoire
de guerre* by Hachette-Jeunesse in 1992

First American edition, 1993

Library of Congress catalog card number: 92-56507

Published simultaneously in Canada by HarperCollins*CanadaLtd*

Designed by Martha Rago

Printed in the United States of America

For Nicolas

"I shall return."

—*General Douglas MacArthur, March 1942*

BACK TO BATAAN

CHAPTER

·1·

IT WAS LATE. I'D HAD A BIG FIGHT WITH MAMA.
She said the Army wouldn't take a soldier who was eleven. I said
I was very mature for my age, and the Army might accept me if
Mama made a special appeal.

"That's ridiculous," Mama said. "Do boys get married at
eleven?"

"No. Not ordinarily."

"Do they become fathers?"

"No."

"Then why should they become soldiers?"

"Because the Army needs young blood."

"Go to bed," she told me. "I don't want to hear such idiotic
remarks."

She wouldn't kiss me good night, or touch my forehead, which
she usually does before I go to bed. I was angry, but I had to

forgive Mama. She works in a factory and Papa is dead. He was killed in the first year of the war. Maybe she thought that one soldier in the family was enough. But I wanted to protect Mama from the Germans and the Japanese. And what was the point of studying and studying if I would end up a soldier in another six years? I might as well be a soldier right now, when my head wasn't ruined by reading so many books.

I went to my room, brushed my teeth, put out all the lights, and called Mauricette.

"Coco, how are you?"

That's my nickname for Mauricette. Coco means "darling" in French.

"Why are you calling me at this crazy hour?" she said.

Mauricette is my fiancée. Mama doesn't know it, but we've been engaged for nine months. I plan to marry her after the war. I would like to have nine children with Mauricette. Nine is a good number, I think. I don't have any brothers or sisters. That's something you should know.

"Mauricette, I'm going to join the Army. And you're the first person I needed to tell."

It was a lie, of course. I'd already told Mama. But you have to lie to your fiancée now and then if you want her to believe in you.

Mauricette started to laugh. "Jack, I can't imagine you as a soldier."

"Why not?"

"You've never been away from home one day in your life. You don't even know what a strange bed is. And what if you had to sleep in the fields? You'd cry all night."

"I wouldn't."

"Yes you would. You can't just call yourself a soldier. You have to train six weeks. That's the minimum."

"I'll train," I said. "And then I'll come back at night to be with you and Mama."

"There's no such thing as a daytime soldier. And if you don't shut up, I'll break off our engagement. I promise you."

It frightened me. I didn't know what I would do without a fiancée.

"Good night, Jack."

"Good night."

I crawled into bed. Suddenly the air-raid sirens started up. I was sure the German planes had come. I peeked through the curtains and saw one of our searchlights crossing the sky. I didn't want anything to happen to Mama. I put on my bathrobe, went into the hall, tiptoed past Mama's bedroom, went out the door, and climbed up to the roof. The sirens were sounding like mad, but there wasn't a single searchlight in the sky. I thought of Papa. I wondered if Heaven had searchlights and soldiers and air-raid sirens.

I thought I could see a German plane in the sky. I wasn't a soldier, but I stayed there, up on the roof. I looked and looked. There was only the black sky. What would I have done if the Germans had come?

The sirens stopped.

I went downstairs to my bedroom. I hadn't woken Mama. I didn't want to lose Mauricette and I didn't want Mama to cry. But one day I would become a soldier. Just you wait and see.

CHAPTER

·2·

Jan. 5, 1943
Jack Dalton
Dutch Masters Day School
Lower Division
New York City
United States

Composition Class
Subject of the Week:
Fathers and Friends

My father died on Bataan in March or April 1942. Nobody knows. The Americans had to run from Bataan, and they couldn't bring his body back, so my father has to lie in a lonely grave on an island that belongs to the Japanese. The Japs don't like prisoners or dead people, soldiers in particular. My mother and my fiancée, Mauricette, don't understand why a boy my age wants to join the Army. But if my fiancée had a dead father, she might understand. I want to be with General MacArthur when he goes back to Bataan . . .

I began to hear giggles from my class and didn't feel like reading any more. I had my own plans with General MacArthur. It didn't concern our class. But they wouldn't stop giggling.

"Jack has a fiancée. Jack has a fiancée."

My teacher, Dr. Franklin, is a very kind man. He wouldn't stick up for the class just because I was a scholarship student and couldn't pay the fees. I'm the little beggar of Dutch Masters Day School. My father didn't own a bank. He wasn't a Hollywood producer. He didn't make soap or tires or hair tonic. He was a soldier who happened to die on Bataan. Jack Dalton. And I was Jack Junior.

"Cut the clowning," Dr. Franklin said.

"What's a fiancée?" asked Arturo Fink, the producer's boy. Arturo is big and fat. He lives with five servants in a mansion on Seventy-sixth Street.

Mauricette was blushing like hell. She sat in the second row. She doesn't like our marriage plans discussed in class. It's a big secret. But I couldn't help myself. I don't like to tell lies in composition class.

"Be a good boy, Jack," Dr. Franklin said, "and enlighten Arturo."

"You can't get married without having a fiancée," I said.

Arturo laughed. "First comes the horse, and then comes the carriage."

Dr. Franklin took him by the ear. "I could expel you, young man."

"No you can't," said Arturo Fink. "My dad is on the school board. He makes donations. He bought the school a library."

It always comes down to the same thing. Arturo's dad. Dr. Franklin let go of Arturo's ear. I don't blame Dr. Franklin. He has to consider his salary.

The bell rang and I was glad. Because I didn't want Dr. Franklin to look bad in the eyes of the class. Sometimes I wonder if Dr. Franklin's on a scholarship, like me. He doesn't have more than a couple of suits, and they're covered with dandruff. He's sitting out the war at Dutch Masters. Dr. Franklin's still a young man, but he has a bad heart. At least that's what Mauricette told me. Mauricette knows everything.

But she wouldn't talk to me after I told our secret. She left the classroom without smiling on her Jack. I could have been the dandruff on Dr. Franklin's coat. I could have been chalk dust. I could have been the last lonesome American cowboy on Bataan.

I had my chores to do. I wiped the inkwells. I wiped the blackboard. I collected all the board erasers. That's what a scholarship boy has to do. I don't mind. It gives me a chance to be with Dr. Franklin after the class is gone.

I wondered about his bad heart. I believed in Dr. Franklin. He'll be here, at the head of the class, clutching the window pole like a lance, if the Japs or the Germans ever arrived on our roof.

"I'm sorry about your dad . . . And congratulations."

"Congratulations?" I said, banging a board eraser against the inside of our garbage barrel.

"You picked a good fiancée."

But I wasn't thinking about marriage. I was thinking of Bataan.

CHAPTER
·3·

MAURICETTE TOLD HARRIET GODWIN I WAS the pig of the class. I had treated her like garbage. Mauricette wouldn't answer my phone calls. She wouldn't read the notes I dropped inside her desk. But Arturo Fink kept reminding her who she was. "Fiancée," he said. "Jack's fiancée."

I promised myself I wouldn't write any more compositions, but how could I graduate from Dr. Franklin's class and join General MacArthur?

It felt lonely without a fiancée.

Mauricette began seeing Barnaby Rosenstock after school. They were holding hands and having chocolate malteds at the Sugar Bowl on Seventy-ninth Street. Fat Arturo was eating two ice-cream sodas. The Sugar Bowl is our hangout. It's the official candy store of Dutch Masters Day School. I didn't have money for ice-cream sodas. I didn't have money for malteds. I'd buy a

Hershey bar or some Chuckles once a week. I'd peek at the comic-book rack and wonder what was happening to Captain Marvel or the Sub-Mariner. Marvel and the Sub-Mariner were already at war, fighting Japs. And when Mauricette was still my fiancée, I'd sit with her over a glass of water and treat her to some candy whenever I could. But now she was sucking malteds with Barnaby Rosenstock. I could hear her from my corner, next to the comic-book rack.

"Oh, Jack Dalton," she said. "He has a wild imagination. He likes to fling words around. He thinks half the school is going to marry him."

She didn't have to shame me in front of her friends. Arturo was laughing into his fat cheeks. Barnaby had a chocolate rainbow on his lips. I didn't even bother with the comic books. Marvel would have to fight the Japs without me. I walked home.

Mama was at the factory. She makes parachutes. Sometimes she'd bring home a little piece of silk left over from one of the chutes. That's how I get my handkerchiefs. Not even Arturo with all his father's money has a handkerchief of genuine silk. But handkerchiefs couldn't make me feel good. Silk is only silk. I wondered about the American fliers who had their planes shot down and had to fall into the dark wearing some of that silk.

I couldn't concentrate on my homework. It didn't seem important when you considered all the Japs and Germans out there. I hope General MacArthur takes me with him to Bataan. I'm not asking for a Purple Heart. I'm only asking to kill Japs. And if I have to die, I want to die near my dad . . .

Mama came home at seven. The streets from my window looked so dark, I thought the world had gone gray. I didn't care. I wouldn't mind going to school after midnight.

"Darling," Mama said, "what's wrong?"

I couldn't tell her how I lost a fiancée, because she would have figured I was insane.

"Mama, I'm blue . . . that's all."

"You're still dreaming of the Army, aren't you? We'll have dinner and listen to the radio, my little blue boy."

We had soup and bread and boiled potatoes and peas out of a can. It's not Mama's fault if meat is rationed and sugar is rationed. No one can inherit ration stamps, not even the President or Arturo's dad.

We listened to Jack Benny. He played the violin and talked about the Japs. Mama laughed, because Jack Benny is the biggest miser in the world. He would never spend a nickel. But he told everybody to buy war bonds.

"What about you, Mr. Benny?"

Mama told me it was time for bed.

I put on my pajamas. But I didn't feel like sleeping. I dialed Mauricette's number and let the telephone ring. Somebody picked up the phone.

"It's me," I said. "Jack Dalton. Your former fiancé. Coco, are you there? I wanted to—"

Mauricette hung up. And I wondered who was lonelier. The dead cowboys on Bataan, or young Jack Dalton.

CHAPTER
· 4 ·

OUR JANITOR AT SCHOOL IS A GERMAN. HIS name is Hans. Arturo is an expert on the Germans. He says Hans has a son in the Luftwaffe and two daughters in the S.S. I didn't believe Arturo. But he went into the basement at Dutch Masters and found a Hitler Cross and part of a German flag. A Hitler Cross isn't like a Purple Heart. It's made of black silver. It's heavy as a hand. It can be given to anybody who has sons or daughters in the German Air Force, Arturo says. I still didn't believe him. Hans is big and mean, and he rules the basement like some rough prince. But Hans never hurt us. He shouts and all that, but he never hurt us.

Arturo showed the Hitler Cross to our principal, Mrs. Caroll. Mrs. Caroll called the FBI. Nothing happened. Hans was as mean as ever. He would eat sandwiches in the dark. The students taunted him, but I took pity on Hans. I didn't think he was a spy.

I'd sit with him on the basement steps.

His neck was always dirty, but janitors can't wash like regular people.

"Mr. Jack," he said, "why they like to talk bad about me?"

"Because talking bad makes them think they're special."

He'd smoke his pipe and then disappear into the dark.

Two men in gray hats arrived at school, went down into Hans's kingdom, and took Hans away. The school rejoiced and Mrs. Caroll wanted to declare a holiday. The trustees wouldn't allow it. They were glad the FBI had come for Hans, but they wouldn't let Mrs. Caroll fool with our calendar.

Arturo started dancing into class. "I caught the spy," he said. Girls kissed him on the cheek. But Dr. Franklin wouldn't give him any gold stars for sneaking into a cellar and stealing Hans's things.

"I deserve five stars," Arturo said.

"You have your arithmetic," Dr. Franklin said, "and I have mine."

"My father's on the school board. I could make you give those stars to me."

"And I could give you extra homework every night of the week."

"You're only a teacher," Arturo said. "My dad's a trustee."

"But he has nothing to do with homework, Mr. Fink. I'm master of the blackboard in this room. I control the stars, silver *and* gold. And you get none."

"But Hans could have murdered me. He's very big."

"Hans never touched you. You know that."

"Why are you sticking up for a Nazi?" Arturo asked.

"If Hans is convicted, Mr. Fink, I'll let you have every gold star in my drawer. Until then, be quiet."

But it looked like Arturo would get his gold stars. Hans was put in a camp on Ellis Island. He seemed to have gone out of our lives. Arturo would smile like a miser and count gold stars in his head. He became more popular than the Lone Ranger or Donald Duck.

He wrote love letters to Mauricette.

He courted her with ice-cream sodas.

She forgot Jack Dalton and Barnaby Rosenstock. She was dreaming of gold stars and the boy who went with them.

I had to comfort my own rival, Rosenstock. He would cry all through composition class. His tears were almost as thick as a finger.

"We were going to get engaged, Jack. After we graduated from Lower Division . . . She jilted me for fat Arturo."

"She's a girl," I said. "She has no sense."

But I had to reconsider.

Arturo had found the Hitler Cross. Hans was in an internment camp. And I couldn't even go out and get Mama a ration stamp.

I was blue for weeks, wondering if General MacArthur would ever go back to Bataan. Arturo's dad came to class. He had polished fingernails and pink hands. His shoes were made of crocodile skin. The handkerchief sticking out of his pocket was as red as a heart. He talked about the lunches he'd had with President Roosevelt. He talked about movie stars. He gave each of us a little card with Gary Cooper's signature. My card read: *To Jack Dalton, the son of a war hero. From the Coop.*

I took the card home to Mama. She cried. She loves Gary Cooper.

"He's Sergeant York," she said. "He's Wild Bill Hickock."

"Mama, it's only the movies."

"Watch your tongue," Mama said. "Don't you say a bad word about Gary Cooper."

Women really don't make much sense. You have to marry them and all that, but they fall in love with movie stars and they think that having Gary Cooper's signature is like having the whole world.

CHAPTER

·5·

ARTURO CAN DO NO WRONG. HE'S PRINCE OF the Sugar Bowl and Dutch Masters Day School. Mauricette is his princess. They have their ice-cream sodas in the afternoon. They giggle in class. Arturo has given her a bracelet. It's solid black silver, like the Hitler Cross. And I have to remind myself: Jack Dalton Junior, you're a fool. If you hadn't mentioned Mauricette in your composition, she'd still be your fiancée.

I miss Hans, to tell the truth. I liked the way he'd come out of the dark to sit with me. He was almost a friend. I wondered how it was to be a spy on Ellis Island. I couldn't believe he had any sons or daughters in the Luftwaffe or the S.S. The FBI had taken him on Mrs. Caroll's word and Arturo's evidence. I had a feeling in my bones that Hans wasn't a spy. Being German was his big crime.

I wrote him a letter.

Dear Hans,

Remember me? I'm Jack Dalton from Dutch
Masters Day. We used to sit and talk until you
got arrested. I hope you're not lonely on Ellis
Island. I think of you a lot.

Your friend Jack

I wasn't sure about Hans's address. I didn't even know his last
name. So I took a chance. I scribbled on the envelope: To Big
Hans, Dutch Masters Day School, c/o the FBI, Ellis Island Camp
Station. I put on a two-cent stamp. And I mailed that letter to
Hans.

Hans never wrote back.

Arturo kept asking about his gold stars. Dr. Franklin looked
him in the eye and said, "I haven't seen a guilty verdict, Mr.
Fink, have you?"

Except for that, the whole class forgot about Hans. He could
have been another dead cowboy on Bataan. Only Hans was German, and he wasn't dead.

Mama had Gary Cooper's signature on the wall. She put the
card in a glass frame. People would come upstairs and visit, just
to see the card. They were practically strangers. And I figured:
Well, if we get poor and run out of ration stamps, I'll sell Gary
Cooper's autograph. But it didn't comfort me. Because Coop had
mentioned my dad. And I wouldn't sell Papa away with any
signature.

I wrote about this in my next composition, but I wouldn't
read it in class. Dr. Franklin was angry. Or maybe he was just
disappointed in his Jack, because I was the best composition

writer at Dutch Masters, Lower Division. I have sixteen gold stars. Arturo doesn't even have seven.

But he read his composition to the class. It was all about his dad and the movies. Arturo talked about lights and cameras and whole gardens that were filled with fake things called props. If you wanted furniture for a movie, like a gravestone or a chair, all you had to do was visit this garden and sign a slip, and the gravestone was yours for a week or a month, however long it took the movie to be made.

I was jealous of Arturo. Not because of the composition. Arturo doesn't have my technique. But he's been inside that garden. He's seen all the chairs and gravestones, and I haven't seen a thing.

And while he was at the Sugar Bowl with Mauricette, a ghost walked into school. It was Hans. He looked all gray and he wasn't so big. He wouldn't say hello to Jack. He disappeared into the basement.

Mrs. Caroll wouldn't comment on the return of Hans. Hans did all his duties. He hammered a lot in the basement. I tried to visit him down there. Hans had his own garden of hammers and saws. He was gloomy.

"What is it you want?"

"Don't you recognize me? I'm Jack."

"I recognize. Mr. Jack, Jack, Jack."

"I wrote you a letter, Hans."

"I'm not receiving Mr. Jack's letter," he said.

I went to the Sugar Bowl and cornered Arturo. He was with his fiancée. I could have been some dead moon to Mauricette. She never looked at me.

"Arturo, we have to talk."

"Later," he said. "We're doing a list for our engagement party. Dad thinks the President might come."

"Arturo," I said, "right now."

Arturo left his ice-cream soda and followed me to the comic-book rack.

"Well, Jack Dalton. Start to talk."

"You framed big Hans, didn't you? That Hitler Cross came out of your father's garden."

"What do you mean?"

"Hans's medal was only a prop."

"You're crazy," he said. His eyes started to roll. He was frightened of Jack. I could have strangled him, but what's the use? I'd only have gone to jail. That wouldn't give Hans back all the hours he spent on Ellis Island, sitting like a spy.

Arturo was my enemy. I didn't care if President Roosevelt and Gary Cooper were on his side.

I walked right out of the Sugar Bowl.

CHAPTER
·6·

I WANTED REVENGE, NOT ONLY FOR HANS. A Hollywood Hitler Cross mocked all the unmarked graves on Bataan. Arturo Fink was fighting a coward's war while soldiers were dying. I wanted revenge.

I didn't have to train. Arturo couldn't even do calisthenics. His belly got in the way. He couldn't climb a rope. He couldn't clutch a basketball. He couldn't run around the bases without falling into the dust and pretending to have a heart attack. He was the only boy in Lower Division who was exempt from PT. He'd made an outcast of Hans, and if he ever married Mauricette, he'd make an outcast of me.

But I couldn't jump Arturo in the dark. I wasn't a German or a Jap. I was an American whose mother made parachutes. And so I challenged Arturo with a personal note. I watched my spelling. I didn't want Arturo to refuse my challenge on account of spelling mistakes. He's a big fat snob. His mother was once the spelling champion of France. She finances all our spelling bees. Mama went to school in a little town upstate, and she couldn't finish college. Her spelling isn't perfect. But I don't care. I'd rather have her as a mother than any queen of the spelling bee.

Arturo Fink, I wrote. *You have wronged Hans. Even if he's German, he's still a human being. Unless you apologize to him in public, in front of Dr. Franklin and our class, please meet me after school on our playing field, near the old horse stable.*

And I signed my name. *Jack.*

I didn't have to be more specific than that. Arturo could remember who I was. I was the only Jack in Lower Division. I dropped the note into Arturo's desk. I kept watching him. He yawned and smiled at his fiancée, Mauricette. He was the proudest fat boy I had ever seen. But he couldn't answer any of Dr. Franklin's questions during our history class.

"Where was Adolf Hitler born?"

"Don't know," Arturo said.

"How old is Mussolini?"

"I can't remember."

"What is Stalin's first name?"

"Jack," Arturo said. Everybody laughed. And then Dr. Franklin started to weave a story about the war. He pointed to Czechoslovakia, a little country on the map of Europe that looked like a wounded peanut, surrounded by Russia, Poland, Germany, Austria, and Hungary. Hitler swallowed that peanut in 1938 and 1939. And he went on swallowing up much bigger peanuts. He swallowed pieces of Poland, a big piece of France. He swallowed up Holland and Denmark and Norway and Greece. I couldn't keep track of all the countries. He was gobbling up Russia, but Hitler had too big an appetite.

"Like Napoleon," Dr. Franklin said, "he can't solve that white riddle of the Russian snow."

"There isn't much snow on Bataan," I said.

It was rude of me to interrupt Dr. Franklin when he was telling us about the German war machine. But he wasn't unkind. "Jack," he said, "Bataan's another story."

I hated Hitler. But I wanted to hear about General MacArthur and Admiral Halsey and President Roosevelt's Pacific fleet. Czechoslovakia was only a peanut. I could feel Bataan in my bones.

I saw Arturo. He was reading my note with his piggly eyes, pondering every word. I could tell. He looked like he had to go to the toilet.

I was glad. I whistled under my breath. I knew he would never show up on the playing field. He could borrow things from his father's garden. But that's about it.

I waited for Arturo. I had to give the fat boy a chance. I watched the horses coming out of the stable. Their hoofs beat on the ground with their own clip-clop. There was a small gang of girls on the horses' backs. They weren't much older than Mauricette. They might have been from Upper Division. But I didn't know Dutch Masters had a riding school. These girls couldn't have been scholarship students like little Jack. They wore expensive red hats, and their boots were made of purple leather with such a polish it could blind you for half a block.

I wondered if MacArthur would bring his own cavalry to Bataan. I wouldn't have minded being a horse soldier, but I didn't know how to ride a horse.

I found Arturo behind me with the Matlocks, Matthew and Paul, those terrible twins of Dutch Masters, Upper Division. They were both football players, and they had muscles on the back of their necks.

Arturo must have bribed them, or they wouldn't have bothered with a Lower Division boy. I prayed the Matlocks wouldn't kill me. I was scared. But it was more than that. A dead boy couldn't get to Bataan.

"Do you have something to say, Jack Dalton?" Arturo asked.

"Yes," I told him. "Yes. You're a rotten liar and your head stinks."

Arturo took all of me in with his piggly eyes. "My head doesn't stink. Take it back."

"You hurt big Hans."

"Take it back."

"Noooooo," I said, and there were spots in my eyes like wild horses who would never live inside a stable.

Arturo punched my face while the Matlocks held me. His fists were like hard paper balls. Arturo was wearing a ring, and the ring cut my mouth. Matthew and Paul didn't say a word. The twins would accept Arturo's money, but they wouldn't talk in our presence. We were nothing but a pair of "low boys."

I saw a string of blood in the air. My blood. Arturo punched and punched. And then an enormous shadow crept between Arturo and me, like a walking wall. It was Hans.

"Why you bother Mr. Jack?"

Matthew opened his mouth. "Go on back to your dungeon, Hansy. This is a school matter. It's none of your business."

"Is my business," Hans said. "Why you help Mr. Arturo? You not in Mr. Arturo's class?"

"We don't have to explain ourselves to janitors," Paul said. "Particularly a Nazi janitor. Heil Hitler, Hans. Go away."

"Heil Hitler yourself."

Paul tried to tackle Hans, but it was Hans who was the real football player. He bumped Matthew with his own body. Matthew fell into Paul. And they both tumbled onto the ground. Fat Arturo ran away. The Matlocks didn't move.

"Come," big Hans said. He brought me to his basement. He had pictures on the walls. I didn't see Hitler's mustache. There was Mrs. Roosevelt in a nurse's uniform. There was Joe DiMaggio in his Yankee stripes. There was a river that could have been the Rhine. But nothing on the walls marked him as a spy.

He searched for balls of cotton and a bottle of iodine. He found the bottle and he dabbed the cuts on my face with little red balls. The iodine started to sting.

"Is nothing," Hans said.

"Hans, you saved my life."

"Is nothing."

The stinging stopped. I was curious as the Devil. "Hans, tell me about the internment camp, please."

"Is nothing," he said.

"Did they have soldiers with machine guns at Ellis Island?"

"Is America," he said. "No machine guns."

And big Hans sent me home.

CHAPTER
·7·

MAMA CRIED.

"Who hit you, Jack?"

"Nobody, Mama. It's a feud, that's all. A little vendetta."

"Vendetta? Should I call Mrs. Caroll? She'll know what your little vendetta is about."

"She's only the principal," I said. "She's practically useless."

"Keep quiet."

"Then don't ask me to explain."

"Go to bed, Jack Junior. You're really an uncivil boy. I breathe silk dust all day. I live around parachutes. And you come to me like a prizefighter, with iodine on your lip. Is that why I send you to a private school? Is that why I slave?"

"I'm a scholarship student," I said. "I clean board erasers."

"Go to bed."

It was dark out, so I didn't mind missing dinner. I pretended it was midnight and brushed my teeth. I shouldn't have talked back to Mama. Parachute dust is lousy for her lungs. She pays Dutch Masters whatever she can. And she gets a little pension from the government. Papa's a war hero, even if he didn't get the Purple Heart. His whole platoon was wiped out, so there wasn't anyone to testify for him and talk about his bravery.

I wanted to write a letter to Papa. I was in a crazy mood. How much postage do you need? Will a two-cent stamp get me to Heaven's gate? I couldn't write the letter. The words wouldn't come. All my composition tricks had failed me.

I listened to the radio. It was a program called the Fat Man, about a private detective. The Fat Man was nimble on his feet. He was always dodging bullets. I heard the opening music. And then the Fat Man climbed on a scale.

"Weight," he said. "Two hundred and forty pounds . . . Fortune: Danger."

That was the Fat Man. But I couldn't concentrate on his travels tonight. He hopped around in the dark. He captured a German spy. The spy's name was Hans. But this Hans wasn't a janitor. He owned a flower shop. And he hid messages inside an orchid. Something like that.

Mama knocked on the door and came into my room. She was carrying a tray filled with carrots and peas and white bread and ham, which was hard to get on account of the war. You had to have a ration book with different-colored stamps. And the grocer could smile on you or not, give you butter and eggs and little extra rations of meat, while he collected the stamps. The grocer is God. He smiled on Mama a lot. He was a bachelor. His name was Mr. Fish. He knew that Papa was buried on Bataan. But he liked Mama, and he wanted to go to the movies with her. This grocer is very rich. But Mama wouldn't go to the movies with him and hold Mr. Fish's hand. She was in love with Papa, even if he's a ghost.

"Mama," I said, "do ghosts ever talk to you while you're asleep?"

"Ghosts? What ghosts?"

"Papa."

"Keep quiet and eat your food."

"I'd like to talk to Papa."

"Papa's dead."

"But he's still a ghost."

"Who told you such nonsense?"

"It's not nonsense. People die and become ghosts. The ghosts walk around at night, because they can't sleep."

"Ghosts," Mama said, and she started to cry again. "That's just a polite word for being nothing at all."

"It's not polite," I said. "It's in the dictionary. Everybody is born with his own spirit. And the spirit doesn't stay in the ground. It walks right out of your skeleton the minute you die."

"Eat your carrots and peas," Mama said. And she left me all alone with my tray. I wasn't hungry. I was thinking about Papa's ghost, and all the other ghosts on Bataan. And I wondered if the Japanese ghosts and the American ghosts ever mingled. What language would they talk? Or do ghosts have a special language? Maybe that's why Papa's ghost hasn't talked to Mama yet. Because ghosts can only talk to other ghosts.

It's funny how much I hated the live Japanese soldiers and didn't hate the dead ones. I imagined them walking around on Bataan, wearing tropical hats, weeping for their sons and their wives. Being dead made them a little human.

I finished the carrots and peas. I finished all the ham. I sank my teeth into the white bread and it tasted like soap. The bread bakers must be in the Army right now. I couldn't fall asleep.

I watched the searchlights outside my window. Silver halos jumped across an endless dark sky. I started to sink all of a sudden. I couldn't keep my eyes open. And that's when I heard the telephone ring. I picked up the phone because Mama was asleep. I recognized Mauricette. But she must have been far away. In Alaska or Bataan. Her voice croaked through the wires.

"I miss you, Jack."

"What about the fat boy?"

"Oh, I'm marrying him for his money."

I was suspicious. "Mauricette, you can't get married when you're eleven. It isn't legal."

"Legal isn't everything, you know."

"But Mrs. Caroll will kick you out of Lower Division."

"She wouldn't dare. No one's allowed to touch a war bride."

"War bride?" I said, whistling through my teeth. "Arturo isn't in the Army."

"He will be. His dad is going to get him into the Hollywood Caravan. He'll entertain all the troops. He'll wear a uniform. He'll sit with Gary Cooper on the train."

I was getting bitter, because Arturo has all the breaks.

"I'm sorry," she said.

"About what?"

"Your face."

"It'll heal. Big Hans bathed all the cuts in iodine. He's like a doctor down there in the basement."

The phone was silent, and then I heard that croak again, like a voice under the water.

"Do you still love me, Jack?"

I couldn't lie. "Yes."

"Do you miss me every hour and every minute?"

"Yes."

"Will you keep calling me Coco?"

"I'll try."

"Will you stay a bachelor all your life when I become Mrs. Arturo Fink?"

"Probably."

How could I promise that I wouldn't fall in love after forty years?

Coco started to cackle like a witch.

"Forty years, forty years."

And I knew this wasn't Mauricette. It had to be the ghost in Mauricette's body that was sitting there until Mauricette died. And the ghost was talking its own crazy talk. It had nothing to do with Mauricette. And it must have come to me in the middle of a dream. Because when I opened my eyes, the searchlights were gone and the sky was all pink. I had to get up and go to school.

CHAPTER
·8·

I'M NOT SURE HOW A COMPOSITION CRAWLS inside your head. But I had to write about the ghosts of Bataan. I read my composition to the class. I had soldiers talking to soldiers, Americans and Japs.

Arturo raised his hand after the reading. "Jack's a pacifist . . . and a traitor to his own dad. If my old man had died in the jungle, I wouldn't sing any praises to the Japs, dead or alive."

Dr. Franklin told Arturo not to call his father an old man.

"But, Dr. Franklin, that's what he calls himself. The old man."

"That's his privilege. You don't have the same privilege in this class."

Barnaby Rosenstock, who was once my rival and was now my friend, said that the War Department wouldn't allow American soldiers to fraternize with the Japs on Bataan or any other island.

"But they're ghosts, Barnaby," I said.

"Then write a better ghost story."

That's how it was, all down the line. Mauricette wouldn't even look at me. Dr. Franklin had to defend my composition. "Haven't you ever heard of sorrow and pity? Jack isn't a pacifist. He's telling us that dead people have their own concerns, and these concerns have nothing to do with the ideas of a nation and national pride."

"Are you a pacifist, Dr. Franklin?" asked Harriet Godwin, and Harriet's very fair.

"No, I'm not a pacifist. I have a heart problem. Or I might have been on Bataan."

But the class didn't have much sympathy for Dr. Franklin or little Jack. I felt like an outcast at the Sugar Bowl. Arturo and Mauricette were celebrating at their own booth. Barnaby Rosenstock had turned his back on me.

"The date is set," Arturo shouted. "The date is set. We'll be officially engaged on March eleventh. My old man is out buying the ring. Mom's doing the invitations. Everybody will get one in the mail."

The invitation arrived the next day. It sat in our mailbox like some magical thing, addressed to Master Jack Dalton. Mr. and Mrs. Burton Fink requested the pleasure of my company at a party in honor of their son Arturo and his classmate Mauricette. But there was nothing about any engagement or engagement rings. Perhaps Mr. Fink was worried about mentioning an engagement between minors in the mail. And then I realized what it was. He was giving a Hollywood party in his mansion on Seventy-sixth Street. It was all make-believe.

I didn't want to go. I wasn't curious about Hollywood on the Hudson (that's where Arturo lives with his mom and dad, right above the Hudson River on the West Side of Manhattan). I wasn't curious about the engagement ring. But I was curious about Mauricette. I could watch her during the party and try to tell if she was really in love with Arturo or was going to marry him for his money, like Mauricette's ghost had said in my dream.

I checked my name in the little black box. Master Jack Dalton was offering the pleasure of his company to Mr. and Mrs. Fink. I put a two-cent stamp on the return envelope and dropped it in the mail. And then I told Mama about the party.

"We'll have to buy you some clothes," she said.

"We can't afford new clothes. Papa's dead."

Mama started to cry.

"I'm sorry, Mama. I didn't mean to hurt you. Can we buy new clothes with a ration stamp? I could start looking for stamps. If I collect enough, we might get a shirt for free."

She laughed a little. "Clothes aren't rationed, silly. It's just hard to find money for them. But we'll manage."

Mama took me to Robert Hall, a men's shop on Broadway that has a lot of bargains. We visited the boys' department. There was a big poster on the wall that showed an American officer with angry eyes and said, "Remember Bataan." I didn't need posters to remind me about my dad. I'm the one who should have had those angry eyes.

Mama bought me a suit at the bargain counter. It was part of the winter sale. Mama used the store's installment plan. The manager gave her a little booklet that allowed her to pay off the price month by month. I wasn't proud of that booklet. It made me feel that I was only renting from Robert Hall. The store owned my suit until Mama got to the last installment. But I didn't say a word.

What did I have to complain about? I had my suit for Arturo's engagement party. Mama ironed my shirt and brushed my shoes. She gave me one of Papa's ties to wear. It had gold and black stripes, and I was happy as hell to wear it. She kept all his clothes in the closet, and sometimes when she felt very bad she'd walk into the closet and hug one of Papa's suits like a crazy person. Only she wasn't crazy. She missed Papa, that's all.

I showed up at the mansion. I hate to admit it, but I was scared, deep down in my belly. I knew I shouldn't have come here. Arturo was my enemy. He always was, long before he stole my fiancée. But it was as if Mauricette's ghost was singing in my ear, tempting me. *Master Jack Dalton, Master Jack Dalton, go inside.*

And I did.

The hallway was bigger than our whole apartment. There were pictures of all the great movie stars, dedicated to Arturo and his dad.

To my silent partner, Arturo, from the Coop.

Gary Cooper, of course. And I was jealous right from the start, before I'd gone a couple of steps into the house.

I stopped reading what Clark Gable and Joan Crawford and Ingrid Bergman had to say. I wasn't a child of Hollywood, like Arturo. And I would never be.

The butler brought me into the living room, which opened onto the river. I felt hypnotized, because I could see the water moving in little white splashy lines that looked like living fingers.

I wondered if a family of giants was walking under the water and could breathe the air with their fingertips. I wished I was part of that family. But it wasn't worth it if I had to lose Mama.

Half my class came rushing into the room with Arturo at the head. He was wearing a sea captain's coat. The buttons were made of gold. He must have taken the kids on a tour of the mansion. He was out of breath, but he had enough oxygen in him to smirk at me.

"Where'd you get the coat, Jack? Is it a leftover from World War I?"

It was clear to me. I'd have to kill him one day. My mother had mortgaged herself to Robert Hall to get me some party clothes for a party that wasn't worth a cent.

"It's brand-new," I said. "From Robert Hall."

And Arturo laughed. "Robert Hall? I wouldn't be caught dead in Robert Hall."

I tried to rush him, but Barnaby Rosenstock held my arms, and when I looked up at Mauricette, I couldn't see much interest for Jack in her eyes. I stopped fighting. I was quiet as a ghost.

I drank punch. I danced with Harriet Godwin and Ruth Malone. I could feel my own spirit climb out of my body and desert Master Jack. I was all alone.

Mrs. Burton Fink brought in the party cake. Arturo took a little velvet box out of his pants. He opened the box. A gold ring was lying in a satin shelf. He picked up the ring with his fat fingers, rubbed the gold, smiled with his moon face, and said, "In the witness of my classmates and this ring, I, Arturo, eleven and a half, promise to marry Mauricette, eleven and three months, at a future date, determined by our parents and ourselves."

It was phony enough. Arturo's mother didn't even have to blink.

And Arturo put the ring on the fourth finger of Mauricette's left hand. That's not how Master Jack would have done it. I would have gotten down on my knees, like a cavalier. I would have fixed the date. The future doesn't mean much in the middle of a war. There is no future for me until General MacArthur goes back to Bataan. I would have left all parents out of the picture. I'd want Mama at the wedding, but not to pick the date. And I would have kissed Mauricette so hard and so long the roots of her hair would have gone all red.

But it was Arturo who had the ring *and* Mauricette. And I had the dust between my toes and a Robert Hall suit that Arturo had scorned.

Mr. Fink came down the stairs with a movie camera. He was wearing a silk scarf. He posed Arturo and Mauricette in front of the cake. The fat boy had his arm around Mauricette. Her eyes were fluttering. She stabbed into the cake with a silver knife. She was the star of the show.

And I felt like a maniac.

Go up the stairs, Master Jack.

I listened to that voice, whoever it was.

I entered a bedroom. It couldn't have been Arturo's. The bed was much too big. I saw President Roosevelt's picture on the wall. He was wearing his sea cape and little eyeglasses fixed to his nose.

He's only a cripple, he's only a cripple, the voice said. It wasn't fair. Mr. Roosevelt came down with polio when he was already a man. Polio is a child's disease. But Mr. Roosevelt got it from swimming in dirty water. Both his legs were asleep and he had to go around in a wheelchair. But he didn't like to be seen in that chair. Hitler called him "that cripple in the White House." That's what Dr. Franklin says. And maybe Hitler was ruling the voice in my head. I didn't care. Germans are Germans and Japs are Japs. There were no Germans on Bataan.

The bedroom had its own little bathroom, and I went inside. I was all crazy and mean. I kept imagining Mauricette with her ring, and Arturo kissing her with his fat lips. Mr. Fink shouldn't have made the movie. I hated Robert Hall. I hated Mr. Fink.

There was a box of tissue paper dug right into the wall. Tissue paper is hard to get on account of the war. I kept pulling that paper from the wall. I stuffed it into the sink, a fat wad of it, like a little mountain.

Light the paper, Master Jack.

I'd never even known I was such a firebug. I couldn't find matches. But I found a cigarette lighter near the sink. It had the initials "C.G." on it. Clark Gable. The whole house was a museum for movie stars.

I snapped the lighter open, flicked the tiny wheel with my thumb until it started to flame up. And then I built a fire right inside the sink.

More ammunition, Master Jack.

I kept feeding paper into the fire. The mirror above the sink turned all black and I looked like the Devil.

The fire started licking the wall. I wasn't satisfied. I threw a towel into the sink. The towel burned almost as fast as the tissue paper.

I left the bathroom. I didn't take the lighter. I wasn't a thief. I was Jack the Devil. But I felt ashamed in front of Mr. Roosevelt's picture.

I went down the stairs.

Everybody was dancing.

I didn't need any butler to take me to the door.

CHAPTER
·9·

IT WAS REFORM SCHOOL OR JAIL, BUT I WASN'T sorry. I was worried about Mama. The police would come to the parachute factory and her face would turn all white when the police told her that the boy she was raising was a firebug and a fiend. Mama works on Saturdays, because the Air Force and the Navy need all the parachutes they can get. It was a quarter to three. I went home. I scribbled a note for Mama. I didn't care about my penmanship or my spelling.

Mama, I set Arturo's father's house on fire. I had to do it. Arturo has everything and he has to suffer.

I signed it, *Your son Jack.*

I had thirty cents in my pocket. It wasn't much of a start. Mama kept her food money in a jar on top of the fridge. I stood on a chair, counted Mama's money, grabbed what I needed, and returned the rest.

I scribbled at the bottom of the note, *P.S. I took three dollars. I'll pay you back.*

I had a little problem being the Devil. I hadn't made any plans. Where would I sleep? How would I ration the money I had? I wasn't a magician. I couldn't make three dollars last and last.

I sneaked down the stairs and started to cry, because I'd never get to Bataan. The Army doesn't take firebugs. I should have considered that. But I still wasn't sorry. The Devil has his own little calendar. And I'd have to learn to follow it.

I could have taken the subway, but I wasn't in the mood to go down into the dark. And I didn't feel like spending a nickel. I needed all the nickels I had. The hoboes had their own little jungle in Riverside Park, and I thought I might borrow a cardboard box from them and use it as a sleeping bag. Papa was always nice to the hoboes. He'd play chess with them and feed them crackers and fruit. When Mama complained about the hoboes being dirty, Papa defended them. He said the hoboes would have stayed clean if they could.

One of the hoboes had carved a good-luck charm for me: it was a wolf's head. You could see the fangs and the eyes. I always kept it in my pocket. I ran down into the park with my wolf's head. It was all the luck I had in this world.

I wasn't going to pray to Papa's ghost in Bataan, not while I was the Devil. I watched the Victory ships in the water. They were carrying war supplies. They'd cross the Atlantic with tons of medicine and ammunition for all the Allied soldiers who sat in England, waiting to jump on Hitler. Dr. Franklin told us it would be a long wait. Hitler had built thousands of little forts along the seawall on his side of the ocean. And I didn't see one fort in Riverside Park. Just an old cannon that some general had put in the park to frighten crows. If the Germans or the Japs ever rode up the Hudson in a submarine, the hoboes would have to defend us.

Their jungle was behind the handball courts. It was like a graveyard that had just been robbed. All the boxes had broken walls. The cans that the hoboes cooked in were squashed into the ground. I saw old shoes and old hats and ripped-up sleeves that lay around like dead elephant trunks. And then someone grabbed me from behind, lifted me into the air, tore out my pockets with all the money I had, and threw me into the rotten dirt of the jungle.

"Mama," I said.

"Shut up."

There were two men standing above me. They were wearing blankets instead of coats. One was very tall and thin. The other was short and thin. Two thin men. The taller one wore three ties to protect him from the cold. He discovered my own tie and pulled it off my neck.

"That's my dad's!"

"Shut up."

The short one had black leather gloves that were ripped along the side.

"Are you with the Patriots?" he asked. "Are you scouting for them? Who are you?"

"Jack Dalton of Dutch Masters Day School."

They both laughed and bowed to me. "Hello, Your Highness."

"I don't understand."

The short one started to squint. "It's a school for little rich kids, ain't it?"

"I'm not rich. I'm a scholarship student. I have to lick the blackboards clean."

"We'll lick you in a minute. We'll lick a hole in your head."

The tall one introduced himself. "I'm Tiny Robert. He's Moose."

The short one, Moose, examined all my money. "You sound rich to me."

"I borrowed most of that from my mother."

"Where's your mother?" he asked. "I'd like to meet the lady."

"She's working," I said. "She makes silk parachutes."

"I'm fond of silk," Robert said.

"So am I," said the Moose. He was clutching my good-luck charm. "Where'd you get that?"

"A man in the park gave it to me. He's my father's friend."

"Moosey," Robert said. "I smell a rat. His Highness is carrying our property. Should we drown him?"

They clutched at me, but a third man came between them. He was wearing a blanket like the other two. But he didn't have their lousy shivering look. He had long eyebrows. He had wavy brown hair. He had a big paunch that swelled under the blanket.

"Jack Dalton, am I your father's friend? Because I whittled that little wolf you had in your pocket."

"I don't remember, sir."

"And your father, what did he have to do with us?"

"He gave you fruit."

"I'm called the Leader. Do you remember me now?"

"No, sir."

"He's lying," Robert said. "You wouldn't accept any fruit from a perfect stranger."

"Don't interject, Robert. I'm having a conversation with the boy."

"Sorry, Leader. I'm sorry."

"Give him his money back. We don't steal from children."

Moose returned my money. He seemed distressed about it. But he wouldn't question the Leader.

"We have to be cautious," the Leader said to me. "The Patriots are after our hides. They call us draft dodgers. But they're wrong. We're invalids, Mr. Dalton. The Moose has a missing lung. Robert has a triple hernia. And my blood pressure's much too high for the infantry. That's why I whittle. It soothes me. Tell me about your dad."

"He died in Bataan," I said.

"That's unfortunate," the Leader said. "But you'll have to explain yourself. We don't usually attract children. Why have you come into our territory?"

"I'm a firebug," I said. "The cops are after me."

"He's an outlaw, Leader," the Moose said. "Like us . . . Sorry. Didn't mean to interrupt."

"I won't ask for details, Mr. Dalton. We're all honorable fellows. But if you've come to live with us, you'll have to share your earthly goods, you'll have to chip in."

He took my three dollars and thirty cents and let me have the little wolf.

But I couldn't have imagined how hard it was to be a hobo. We packed the cardboard boxes and the tin cans and carried them on our backs. The Leader had to keep changing our campsite to avoid the Patriots and the police.

"Pardon, Leader," the Moose said. "But I don't trust this kid.

He comes in out of nowhere, and you tolerate him, take him into the fold."

"Mr. Moose, I remember his dad. I played chess with him. He always favored the black pieces . . . a peculiar man."

"Why didn't you say so?" Robert asked.

"I say what I want when I want to say it. I'm the Leader."

We trekked up the spine of Riverside Park to another campsite, which was the wading pool of an abandoned playground. The back wall of the pool was our windbreaker.

The Leader could build the loveliest fire in a tin can. We had hot dogs wrapped in white bread and applesauce that we ate out of a jar. He roasted potatoes in our cans, and we had them, too. The Leader let me have the biggest potato.

The moon had come out from behind the trees. It shone like the Devil. The Leader gave me a blanket and a stick.

"The stick is for rats, Mr. Dalton. If they start to nibble on your feet, well, you wallop them once. They'll go away."

After Robert fell asleep, the Leader unraveled Papa's tie from around Robert's neck and gave it to me.

"He's a child," the Leader said. "He has a craziness for neckties."

Soon as I was settled in my own box, I asked, "Leader, do you really remember my dad?"

"I do. He was the kindest sort of man. He never judged us. He played chess, he offered us food, but it wasn't charity, Mr. Dalton. It was simple respect . . . Now good night."

"Aren't you going to sleep?"

"I never sleep at night, Mr. Dalton. It would be a dangerous habit. I taught myself to sleep while I'm walking. It's much safer. You might stumble, but you won't get kicked in the head."

I moved down into the box. I had my blanket and my stick and Papa's tie. I missed Mama, but I wasn't lonesome. I had the Leader and his two big hobo children. I was lucky, and I don't think it had much to do with the Devil. Papa had adopted the hoboes in his own way, and now the hoboes were adopting me.

I closed my eyes and had the calmest sleep you could ever have inside a cardboard box.

CHAPTER
·10·

THE LEADER BOILED WATER IN A TINY BOTTLE
and we all brushed our teeth. Then we had our morning "beverage," with the Leader taking a tea bag and dunking it into our
tin cups. He made the law. We had to get out of the playground,
because the park had its own police, and the police liked to visit
this playground at 9 a.m. and handcuff whatever hoboes they
could find. We packed our gear and ran off into the woods. The
Leader had memorized everybody's timetable. He could make us
invisible if he had to.

He brought us to a cave under the old Riverside Park baths.
The baths had been shut down because they drank up too much
water. We could sit in the stone cave until around noon, when
the police broke for lunch. They wouldn't come back. They'd
sleep in the afternoon and patrol the upper half of the park. The

Leader told us stories while we sat in the dark. They weren't pieces of fiction. They were facts out of his own life. He'd been a detective and a cowboy and a gambler in all the big capitals of Europe.

"Did you ever gamble in Germany, Leader? In Berlin?"

"I did."

I had to ask him. "Did you ever meet Adolf Hitler?"

"Yes. He wasn't a dictator then. He was a rabblerouser in a torn shirt. He painted his mustache so it would shine. He had a hole in his shoe. His neck was dirty. We were at a small café. He was covering up the cracks in his leather coat with shoe polish. I'm not sure why, but I bought him a cup of coffee and some strudel. He was like a little monk with crazy eyes."

"Pardon, Leader," Robert said, "but are you sure it was the original Adolf? I mean, there must have been Hitler look-alikes."

"It was Hitler," the Leader said. "I've seen that face again and again at the movies, in the March of Time."

"Leader, I hear he hired a double and sent him into the streets of Berlin to sit at cafés and beg apple strudel from foreign gamblers and other strangers."

I heard a slap in the dark. Robert began to cry. "But it's possible, ain't it? Stalin has a double. So why shouldn't Adolf Hitler have one?"

"Because he couldn't afford a double. He had to spend his money on shoe polish. Shut your mouth."

And we fell into silence until the Leader said, "Children, it's noon. Time to leave the cave."

I'm ashamed to admit it, but after a day with the Leader, I had no other life. I didn't forget Mama, and I thought about Bataan, but the world outside Riverside Park crept into the shadows. I had my box and my blanket and my fire can.

I was Mr. Dalton, friend and mate of Robert, Moosey, and the Leader. I learned as quick as I could. I baked my own potatoes in the storm of a tin can. I could shut my eyes and sleep for a couple of seconds in the middle of a march. But I could never in a million years strike the head of a kitchen match and get it to flame in one perfect red feather, like the Leader could. He was a genius.

But he couldn't make money out of water and grass. He had to steal. Hoboing wasn't as cheap as you think. We had fixed expenses, the Leader liked to say. Hot dogs and potatoes and cigarettes, candy bars and sweet peas, because we had to have some vegetables in our diet. And *The New York Times*, which the Leader held between his fists like some precious thing. He knew as much about current events as Dr. Franklin did.

"Mr. Dalton, there's no paper on the planet like *The New York Times*. It's one of God's gifts."

"Nothin' to do with God," thin Robert muttered. "And don't ask me to beg your pardon. A paper's a paper, that's all. It delivers news. It has pictures and a society page. It says who was born and who died."

"Shut your mouth," the Leader said. "I couldn't live without the *Times*. I'd be one more tramp in Riverside Park. But I can go to India every morning. I can study Singapore . . . and Bataan. I haven't forgotten your father, Mr. Dalton."

He recited the whole history of Bataan and Manila Bay, how Ferdinand Magellan discovered the Philippines in 1521 and decided it was part of the New World, how the Filipinos didn't like being discovered and killed Magellan, how the Spanish conquered the Filipinos in 1564, how the Americans kicked out the Spanish after the Spanish–American War, how the Japs crept onto the islands in a bunch of sneak attacks and ran off General MacArthur.

It was a wonderful portrait of the Philippines and Bataan, and I realized that this hobo who loved *The New York Times* was the best teacher I had ever had. He'd rush out of the park around 1 a.m., while the rest of us were asleep, and take his *Times* off a delivery truck. And he'd read his paper through the night, scanning pages in the dark and keeping alert to any suspicious noise, because it would have been fatal if our enemies ever found us.

We lived off Mama's food money for an afternoon, and then the Leader had to return to his old habit of raiding little vendors' shacks that were distributed throughout the park. He would snap off a vendor's lock with his own fingers and steal small parcels of food.

"Leader," the Moose would cry, "take it all, take it," as he stared at long strings of frankfurters and cigarette cartons and boxes of candy bars.

But the Leader was much wiser than the Moose. He knew how much "leakage" the vendors would tolerate without going to the police or the Patriots.

We couldn't get our potatoes and sweet peas out of a vendor's barrel. We had to swipe them from one of the Victory Gardens that the War Wives of Riverside Park had planted. Mama was a War Wife, but she didn't have time to tend her own garden. She was breathing silk six days out of seven. The President's wife,

Eleanor, had started the War Wives. The Republicans didn't like Mrs. Roosevelt. They called her horseface. I didn't care. She was the kindest horseface in the world.

The War Wives had their gardens up on the hill, near Riverside Drive. We'd scout the gardens just before dark, when there weren't any Wives around. The gardens had their own keeper, but he was a lazybones, and he liked to sleep with a hat over his eyes. Robert would crawl under the wire fence while we kept watch. He'd pluck sweet-pea plants and pull potatoes from the ground, put them into a little sack the Leader prepared from pages of the *Times*, and then crawl back out to us.

It was pilfering from these gardens that got the Patriots angry, and they swore to make us suffer. I still didn't understand. "Who are the Patriots, Leader? Men or boys?"

"It's hard to tell. They wear masks. But don't worry. You'll see them soon enough."

All I saw was a woman enter the gardens. She didn't look much like a Patriot. She was carrying a hoe and she began to dig around in the dark. I recognized her face. It was Arturo's mom. I was happy and sad at the same time. She could have perished in the fire. Only what about the others? Mr. Fink and Arturo and Mauricette? Barnaby Rosenstock and the butler? And the rest of my class? Suppose I had killed them?

A firebug had to take full responsibility for his fire.

I started calling out to Mrs. Fink, but the Leader put his hand over my mouth.

"One more peep, Mr. Dalton, and there'll be consequences."

I whispered when he took his hand away. "That's Mrs. Fink. She was part of the fire I made. I wanted to ask her about—"

"Enough, Mr. Dalton. A real firebug would have more control. He wouldn't get sentimental about any of his fires. That woman can tattle on us. She could be a hazard to our health."

"Yes, Leader. You're right, Leader."

And I followed him away from the Victory Gardens.

CHAPTER
· II ·

I HAD A DREAM THAT NIGHT.

It wasn't about Mrs. Fink or the fire. Mrs. Roosevelt appeared in my dream. She was on the porch of the White House, all alone. She started digging into the floor with her own hands. Then her hands started to bleed. There must have been a garden right under the porch. She pulled out potatoes and radishes with all the roots. And she fell through the hole in the floor.

I screamed.

The Leader pulled me out of my box. Pages of the *Times* were around his knees.

"Nothing to worry about, Mr. Dalton. Shake it off. It's only a bad dream. I have them all the time."

"While you're walking, Leader?"

"Yes. While I'm walking. That's why I trip. When I'm coming out of a dream."

But it wasn't much consolation. I kept seeing Mrs. Roosevelt's bloody hands, and I knew some harm would come to us.

The Leader boiled some water so we could brush our teeth.

I heard the crackle of sticks.

I saw those masks, two by two, party masks that didn't cover much. I recognized them by their shoulders, bobbing and bouncing with that familiar swagger of the Dutch Masters football team. These were Upper Division boys, with the Matlock twins up front, Matthew and Paul.

"The Patriots, the Patriots," Robert screamed, and ran out of our campsite with the Moose.

These Patriots paddled their behinds with big fat sticks, but they weren't concerned about capturing Robert and Moosey. They wanted the Leader.

They formed a circle now. The Leader might have broken through, but he wouldn't have left me all alone.

"Steady, Mr. Dalton," he said, holding me against his thigh, like some bear cub. The Patriots charged with their sticks. The Leader dodged their blows. He struck back with his fists. The Patriots fell around him, rolled in the grass, and got up again.

There was blood in the Leader's eye.

Matthew took off his mask. "Hello, little Jack. How are you?"

The Leader looked at me and Matt. He had such disappointment on his face.

"Robert's right," he said. "You are their spy."

"Nooooo," I said, but the Leader wouldn't listen. He shoved the Patriots out of the way and went off into the woods, hugging his own bruised body.

I tried to follow him. But the Matlocks picked me up, smiled, and said, "How's the little firebug?"

I was too discouraged to cry.

The Patriots carried me out of the park and into the halls of our school. They hid their masks and sticks and presented me to Mrs. Caroll.

"Look at you," she said, shoving me right into the mirror.

My face was covered with dirt. I had twigs in my hair. My coat was ruined. My pants were ripped. Papa's tie was full of dark spots.

"Jack Dalton," she said, "you are an evil boy."

I kept thinking of the Leader and how I'd hurt him. It wasn't my fault. I couldn't help it if the Patriots were all from Dutch Masters.

Faces kept peering through the glass in Mrs. Caroll's door. I recognized Arturo and Mauricette. I wasn't even glad they were alive.

A man came into the office. He was wearing a raincoat and a big hat. He took out a little leather case with a gold badge inside. "Detective Bruno Wicks. I'm from the Burglary Squad."

Mrs. Caroll wasn't frightened of any badge.

"Detective, my school board advised me to call the police. But you aren't going to arrest him, are you? The boy isn't even twelve. He's disgraced himself, he's done terrific damage, but he's still in my charge . . . until I take him off our rolls."

"Please, Mrs. Caroll . . . let me talk to him."

"Without a witness?"

"You can take down my badge number . . . I wouldn't touch a kid."

And Mrs. Caroll abandoned me to Detective Bruno Wicks. He lit a cigarette and blew smoke rings into the air and scattered them with his hand.

"Would you like a cig?"

"I'm not allowed to smoke."

He shaped one of the rings into a woman's body.

"I call her Clara. She's all hips . . . I learned that at reform school. I was a runt like you. Ten or eleven. Now tell me what happened?"

"I was at Mr. Fink's mansion on Seventy-sixth Street."

"Wait a minute."

He took out a notebook and started to scribble. He mumbled, "Mansion . . . Seventy-sixth."

"Arturo insulted me. I went upstairs. I made a fire in the bathroom sink."

"Is it the first time you ever torched a place?"

"Yes. The only time."

"And then what happened?"

"I walked home, borrowed three dollars from my mother's money jar, and went into the park."

"A cool customer," Wicks said. "Go on."

"I met the Leader and two of his friends."

"The Leader?"

"He's a hobo."

"Does he look like this?" Wicks asked, taking a photo out of his pocket. It was the Leader as a younger man, wearing a convict's shirt with numbers across his chest. "Is that him?"

"Yes."

"His name is Harvey Winters White. He was sent to prison for burglary and assault. And you say he's been nesting in Riverside Park, playing the hobo."

"He is a hobo. He's been a hobo for years. Before that he was a detective and a cowboy and a gambler in Berlin."

"That's a laugh. He just got out of Sing Sing."

"It isn't true. He played chess with my father."

"When?"

"Three years ago."

"Did you see them play?"

"I'm not sure. But he gave me this." I took the wolf out of my pocket. "He whittled it, carved it with his own hands."

Wicks grabbed my wolf away. He put it into a little bag.

"That's mine," I said.

"Not anymore. It's police evidence. But you'll get it back . . . after we tag it. Now what did Harvey steal when you were with him?"

"Nothing," I said.

"What did he steal?"

"A few hot dogs to keep alive. And some potatoes and peas from a Victory Garden."

"That's a start," he said. "I'll write this all down and I'll need you to sign the report . . . in front of Mrs. Caroll or a police matron."

"I won't sign," I said.

"You will. I'm not letting old Harvey get away. He's tricked me twice. He hides out with the hoboes between jobs. He's a major thief."

"I won't sign."

"Then we'll take a nice little walk to children's court. We'll see what the judge has to say."

"I don't care. The Leader's my friend."

I heard the glass rattle in Mrs. Caroll's door.

Mr. Fink walked in. His face was all red. I thought he was going to kill me. But he asked Detective Wicks, "What is this?"

"Nothing, sir. Just a little chat." He flicked out his badge. "Wicks, Bruno Wicks."

"The boy hasn't seen his mother yet. Why are you interrogating him?"

"I'm a policeman, sir. Who are you?"

"Burton Fink."

"He torches one of your rooms and you're angry at me?"

"He's a child. Not a criminal. I'm taking him to his mother. Goodbye, Detective Wicks."

He brought me out into the hall. Students kept staring at me. I went to the water fountain with Mr. Fink. He lent me a handkerchief and I washed my face.

There was a limousine outside school with a chauffeur and all. It was the kind of car Presidents and Hollywood producers would have. The chauffeur climbed out and opened the door for us. He was wearing a cap with a polished bill, like an Army Air Force pilot, only this bill was black.

We sat on tall cushions, like two kings.

"Gas is rationed," Mr. Fink said. "I have to share my chauffeur with four other men . . . but this was an emergency."

"I'm sorry about the fire, Mr. Fink."

"It wasn't serious. A broken mirror and a few blisters on the wall. But you shouldn't have run away."

"I was scared."

"You shouldn't have run away. I got the truth out of Arturo. I didn't know that Mauricette had been your friend before she was Arturo's. It was foolish of me to give him such a party, with a ring for Mauricette . . . and I ought to spank you for trying to destroy my house. But I can't. I'm not your father."

We drove into Queens, where Mama's factory is. She came

out of the big factory room, wearing her smock and big round hat that are supposed to gather all the silk dust. She was laughing and crying. She hugged me and pinched me until the dust fell on my face.

"I don't know how to thank you," she said to Mr. Fink. "I'll pay for the damages Jack did."

"Please, we won't talk about that . . . Some of the older boys at school went on an expedition and found him in the park."

"They didn't find me, Mr. Fink. They call themselves the Patriots. They beat up hoboes. They didn't find me."

I'd made him angry. He had splotches on his cheeks. "I don't see how you can say that, Jack. I asked the Matlock twins to look for you. And they did . . . as a special favor."

"They were wearing masks. They had sticks."

"Shhh," Mama said, and she dug my face so deep into her smock I was breathing nothing but silk. I don't care. I'd lost the Leader.

CHAPTER
·12·

MRS. CAROLL WANTED TO THROW ME OUT OF
Dutch Masters, but she didn't dare. Mr. Fink is our benefactor.
He pays most of the school's bills. And so I was put on probation.
I had to visit the school psychologist twice a week. Her name is
Mrs. Stone. She had an office near the roof. I'd climb up to the
attic and sit with her for half an hour.

She'd give me tests with inkblots and different colors. I'd close
my eyes for her, and she'd ask, "Jack Dalton, what's the first thing
you see?"

"Harvey Winters White, the Leader."

"Where is he?"

"Lying on the ground, ma'am. The birds are pecking out his
eyes."

"Do you hate the Leader?"

"No, ma'am. I loved him."

"Then why do you wish him dead?"

"It's not a wish, ma'am. The Patriots want him dead. They're all members of our football team. They hate hoboes."

"And you really think there's a gang of Upper Division boys who roam the park as vigilantes?"

"What's a vigilante?"

"Someone who's above the law, who decides on his own what's right."

"They're vigilantes, ma'am, and worse."

"That's a harsh judgment against your own schoolmates, particularly when they rescued you from the park."

"They didn't rescue me, ma'am. They stole me from my friends."

"Your friends? Harvey Winters White was in the penitentiary. He might have harmed you."

"He wouldn't. He's the Leader. He taught me how to roast a potato in a tin can."

"He took your mama's money."

"I took the money, ma'am. I gave it to the Leader. It's share and share alike. That's how a hobo lives."

"You're not a hobo."

"I am."

"You're a boy at Dutch Masters. You have a future."

"If I can't go to Bataan, I might as well live in the park."

"You aren't making much progress, young Jack. How can I take you off probation if you talk like that?"

"I'm only telling the truth, ma'am."

"You've hurt the people who care for you. You've been a renegade. Think about the life you want to squander on a madman in the park. And come back to me with a better attitude."

"I will, ma'am."

But I had no better attitude. It was clear as a bell. I was a
hobo pretending to be a student at Dutch Masters. I lost my
composition skills. Barnaby Rosenstock got the gold stars. I was
a ghost. I didn't even have the Devil to comfort me. Mauricette
was wearing her engagement ring. She'd polish it all afternoon
until Dr. Franklin obliged her to take it off.

Dr. Franklin asked me questions that bounced right off my
skull. I felt like a mummy, wrapped inside a lot of cloth. I stayed
after school, washing Dr. Franklin's notes off the blackboard.

"Where are you, Jack? You're not in this class."

"Don't you know, Dr. Franklin? I'm the firebug."

"What on earth happened at Arturo's party?"

"I heard the Devil. He told me to walk upstairs and build a
little fire."

"Tell me more about the Devil."

"There's nothing to tell. He was inside my head. I listened to
him. And I became the Devil for a little while."

Dr. Franklin helped me scrub the blackboard.

"You must be a scholarship student," I said. "Like Jack Dalton."

"No. My best student has run away from me. I want him
back."

I didn't know what to say. I could see how sad he was over his
fallen star. But school didn't mean much after studying with the
Leader. I'd had my kindergarten and my college in Riverside
Park.

I trusted Dr. Franklin. He was the only person I'd ever told
about the Devil. But I couldn't learn from him.

I went out into the cold. The football team was practicing in their field. The team practiced all year long, summer and winter. They were the regional champs. They'd walloped every other day school in New York, Connecticut, and New Jersey. Recruiters from all the big football colleges would sit in the stands and watch them play. The Matlocks already had football scholarships. Paul will go to Harvard, and Matthew will go to Yale. They looked gruesome in their shoulder guards. But they could gallop like horses and get a football to fly like an impossible bird.

They didn't have to bother with a firebug. They'd returned me to Dutch Masters, and now I was invisible to them. There could never be any relationship between the Upper and Lower Divisions. That's a fact of life.

I saw big Hans sitting outside his basement, sucking on a pipe.

"Hello, Mr. Jack," he said.

"Hello, Hans."

"I'm glad you come home to us."

"School isn't a home," I said. "My home is with the hoboes in Riverside Park."

"Is foolish, Mr. Jack. Hoboes? You have education. You could live in the White House one day."

"And be married to a horseface?" I don't know why I said that. I liked Mrs. Roosevelt.

Hansy was hurt. He had Mrs. Roosevelt's picture in the basement. But I couldn't help myself. I was like a lonesome monster who could only spit yellow blood and say terrible things. I'd crossed over the border into some wilderness. It was the land of no return.

CHAPTER
·13·

I STOPPED LISTENING TO THE RADIO. I DIDN'T care about Jack Benny or the Fat Man. I ate what Mama fed me. I did my chores. I'd steal *The New York Times*, hide it under my bed, and read it when Mama wasn't around. I got my satisfaction knowing that Harvey Winters White was reading exactly what I read. I felt close to the Leader. I studied Stalin and General de Gaulle, who wanted to free all of France. I read about Mrs. Roosevelt, who visited coal miners in the caves of Pennsylvania, bringing them chocolate and masks to wear against all the black dust.

Forgive me, Eleanor.

That wasn't the Devil. It was Jack Dalton.

I read about Joe Louis, the heavyweight champion of the world, who visited Harlem on his vacation from the Army. Joe Louis is a black man who beat up Max Schmeling, Hitler's favorite fighter.

That's what it said in the *Times*. Hitler believed in a master race of blue-eyed darlings. The Leader doesn't have blue eyes. I don't. Mama doesn't. And neither does Joe Louis.

And suddenly I had the itch to write a composition. About blue eyes and all the trouble they have caused. But the words wouldn't come.

Mama came home. I hid the *Times*. We talked.

"I'm worried, Jack. You never smile . . . You've changed since you were in the park."

"Mama, things happen. I was gone a whole week."

"No," she said. "Four days and three nights."

"Four? It felt like seven."

"You could invite your hobo friends for dinner."

"They wouldn't come. They're outlaws."

"Oh, my Jack," she said. "I can't give you a father. He's gone . . . Don't you love me a little?"

"I love you, Mama. I love you a lot."

"Then what's wrong, baby?"

"I miss the Leader, Harvey Winters White."

"You promised," Mama said. "You promised you wouldn't go back into the park by yourself."

I did promise Mama. It was bad enough she had to breathe silk dust all day without worrying about Jack Junior.

"I'll go with you to the park," she said. "On Sunday."

But I'd die if the Leader caught me in the park with my own mother, walking around like a little boy.

"It's all right, Mama."

"It's not all right. I've neglected you, Jack."

"No you haven't. You work like a dog."

"Stop that! Every parachute I make will help win the war."

"But the silk dust will get in your lungs and you'll start to cough. And then you'll live in a sanitarium. And I'll have to bring you sandwiches. It's not worth it, Mama."

"Our soldiers are dying. I have to help . . . I'm one of the War Wives. I'll ask for a little plot of land, and we'll go gardening together."

"But I don't know how to garden."

"We'll learn," she said.

Mama was as stubborn as a mule.

We got our hoe from the War Wives equipment bureau, we got our piece of garden, and Mama bought seeds and onion bulbs and fertilizer that was black as midnight. And we went to the Victory Gardens. Mama showed her permit to the gatekeeper, and he let us in and escorted us to our plot. It looked like an unmarked grave, because nothing was growing in it. But we put down sticks to hold the sweet peas when they started to climb. Mama chopped at the earth, and we planted all our seeds and bulbs.

We weren't alone in the Victory Gardens. The gardens were filled with War Wives, a few of their husbands, and some of their kids. It was like a Sunday picnic in Riverside Park. Mr. and Mrs. Fink were there, without Arturo. They offered sandwiches to Mama and me. I ate mine with a miserableness in my heart. It was Mr. Fink who paid for my scholarship at Dutch Masters. He rescued me from that detective in the raincoat. He brought me to Mama's factory with the little bit of gas he had left in his limousine. And all I ever did was try to burn his house.

I gardened with my nose in the ground.

And when I looked up, Mauricette was there with her own mom, gardening right next door, only the Victory Gardens didn't have any doors. I couldn't avoid Mauricette. She said "Good morning" to Mama, and she walked over to Jack the gardener. She had a hoe in her hand, but she wasn't wearing her engagement ring.

"Can I talk to you, Jack? In private."

"I'm busy," I said. "I have to watch my potato crop."

"You don't have any potatoes yet."

"Well, I'm trying," I said.

Mama tapped me on the shoulder. "Be polite."

And I walked with Mauricette to some neutral ground between her mother's plot and mine.

"Talk," I said.

"Will you give me a chance to breathe, for God's sake?"

"Where's your ring?"

"I gave it back."

"Changing partners again?"

"You always think the worst, Jack Dalton. You weren't such a pessimist when you asked me to marry you."

"That was a million moons ago."

"It was not. It was right before Christmas."

And I couldn't help it. Mauricette was gorgeous in her blue gardening clothes. My knees began to knock from looking at her.

"I apologize," she said. "I behaved like a witch. I don't love Arturo. I never did."

"Arturo took the ring off your finger, didn't he?"

"Almost," she said. "It was his father's idea. Mr. Fink said we should never have had an engagement party. It was the party that turned you into a firebug."

"Not at all," I said. "I was a firebug without ever knowing it. The party gave me my big chance."

She started to cry and I wanted to kiss her in front of all the War Wives.

"You're cruel, Jack Dalton."

"A hobo has to live by his wits."

"You disappeared into the park and you came out wild . . . We had a secret, Jack. I was your fiancée and you had to write about it in one of your compositions. You had to tell the whole class."

"If it was so embarrassing," I said, "why'd you get engaged to Arturo?"

"Jack," she said, "you're a moron, like every other man."

And she went back to her mom's little garden.

CHAPTER
·14·

I BEGAN GETTING MY GOLD STARS AGAIN.
Blame it on *The New York Times*. I could answer every question
Dr. Franklin asked about the war and the world. I had all the
facts and figures in my head.

"Class, what's the relationship between potatoes and World
War II?"

I raised my hand.

"The people of Europe would be dead without the potato. The
Germans have taken all the chickens and the cows. They've stolen
cheeses from the Dutch, the French, and the Polish people. But
the people are fighting back. They're growing potatoes in their
own private gardens . . . on the roofs of Amsterdam and Paris.
In the back yards, near the outdoor toilets. And sometimes in the
toilets themselves. They eat the potato, turn the potato into sugar

and alcohol, candy and bread, and they guard the skin, because the skin is precious. They make false coffee out of it. They make padding for their quilts and their clothes. They freeze it until it's like bark, and chew on that bark all winter."

The whole class looked at me with goggly eyes.

"That's stupendous," said Barnaby Rosenstock.

And Dr. Franklin was proud as hell. Because he knew that at least some of my spirit had come home to Dutch Masters. Jack was Jack. But I was only reciting what I'd picked up from *The New York Times*, with a little embellishment, like the Leader would do. I was only following the Leader.

The class was ready to lick my shoes. Even fat Arturo, who was falling behind in every subject.

"Will you tutor me, Jack? My dad will pay you fifty cents an hour."

"I'll think about it," I said.

Mrs. Caroll learned how I'd become a wizard, and she canceled my probation. I didn't have to meet in the attic with Mrs. Stone. I was put on the Honor Roll. I had more gold stars than anyone in the Lower Division. But I couldn't seem to satisfy Mauricette.

I offered to study with her, help her with her homework.

"No thanks," she said. "I can survive without such a genius."

"I'm sorry if I sounded bitter," I said. "But I couldn't bear it when you put on Arturo's ring."

"I didn't think hoboes bothered themselves about engagement rings."

"I'm not a hobo anymore."

"It's a pity," she said. "I liked you better when you were a wild man."

You just can't win. I was crazy about Coco and Coco was crazy about me, I imagine, but we were closer to being enemies than friends.

I'd see her on Sundays at the Victory Gardens.

I'd start hoeing, with all the other War Wives nearby. They'd look at Mr. Fink, and they must have been a little jealous, because husbands were scarce in the garden. They were either dead, like Papa, or living in a foxhole, like Mauricette's dad.

I couldn't draw her attention, no matter what I did. I'd dance with the hoe, pretending it was Ginger Rogers, but Mauricette wouldn't even notice. And I wondered how I could win her back. I missed the phone calls we'd had. Mauricette used to teach me French. Her mom wasn't born in Paris, like Mrs. Fink. But she lived there five years. She was once a fashion model. I saw pictures of her in silk gowns that made her look like Cinderella. Her mom would say, *"Paris me manque."*

It means Paris misses her. Something like that. I was hoping that Mauricette and me would have our honeymoon in Paris. But not with the Nazis around. I wouldn't want to live on potatoes all the time.

Mama was thirsty. She handed me two dimes. "Buy me some orange soda, Jack. And you can treat Mauricette."

"Mama," I said, "she wouldn't drink soda out of Jack's hand."

"Shush! And don't dillydally. You're carrying twenty cents."

I went out the garden gate. But I didn't have any luck. My old friends found me before I could find the soda man. They rushed at Jack Dalton from behind a tree. Robert and the Moose, with miserable red eyes, and wearing their blanket coats. Robert was clutching a knife.

He whisked me under his blanket.

"Don't you scream, little man. I'll slaughter you like a chicken."

"Where are we going?" I shouted into the wool of the blanket.

"To the Leader."

CHAPTER
·15·

I WAS SCARED AND EXCITED AND A LITTLE crazy. I'd promised Mama I'd come right back, but I wouldn't miss the chance of being with the Leader.

I couldn't see where the hell we were going. I had wool in my eyes. I kept bouncing up and down under the blanket until I thought I was a piece of Robert, a great big bubble of skin. And then Robert dropped me onto the ground.

The Leader was standing above me. He had the same red eyes as the other two. He was looking grim. He had little nicks in his eyebrows. His wavy hair was gone. It was all in knots. He had stubble on his chin. And there was such contempt in his eyes that I could tell I'd never have the privilege of being a hobo again, not even for a minute.

"I didn't betray you, Leader. I swear on all the American graves in Bataan."

We were in the woods north of the Victory Gardens. I recognized the place. It was one of our camping grounds.

"This is a court of inquiry," the Leader said. "I'm the judge. Robert and Moose are the jury."

"But, Leader, I can explain."

"Shut your mouth, Mr. Dalton. You'll have your chance. I have to address the jury."

The Leader stood with his hands behind his back, his paunch sticking out. He could have been a pirate. Humbled as I was, at his feet, I was still proud of him.

"Gentlemen of the jury, this child comes to us out of the blue, begging for assistance, swearing that he was a firebug who needed a home, and did we deny him?"

"No," said the two thin men, hoboes and members of the jury.

"He showed us an animal, a carved fox—"

"Leader," I said, "it was a wolf."

"I stand corrected. A whittled wolf that one of the vagrants had given him in gratitude for a certain kindness to these very vagrants. And didn't we welcome him?"

"We did," said Robert and the Moose.

"And didn't we discover, much to our chagrin, when the Patriots were upon us, that those obnoxious masked men were known to him, that they winked into his very eyes?"

"Yes."

"And isn't it a likely conclusion that the masked men used Mr. Dalton as a decoy, that they sent him into the park to seek us out and lure us into their own filthy trap?"

"Yes, Leader, yes."

"What's your verdict, then?"

"Guilty as charged."

And the Leader looked at me with that rawness in his eye. "You'll have to suffer the consequences, Mr. Dalton."

"It isn't fair. I didn't know that the Patriots were members of Dutch Masters' football team. They're not friends of mine. I don't exist for them. They wouldn't even say hello to me."

"They said hello. I heard them," said the Leader.

"That's because Mr. Fink paid them a reward to catch me."

"Who's Mr. Fink?"

"The man whose house I tried to burn."

"Tell him the consequences," Robert said. "Tell him."

"Ten dollars a week."

"What ten dollars?"

"The ten dollars that's going to provide for our support, that's going to keep us from perishing."

"It might as well be a million. Where would I ever get ten dollars a week?"

"Steal," said the Leader.

"I'm not a thief."

"Then you'll have to educate yourself to be one, because we'll burn down your mama's garden, we'll burn down your school, we'll burn down Mr. Fink."

I was beginning to lose respect for the Leader. "I'll bet you would, Mr. Harvey Winters White."

The Leader blinked. "Who told you that name?"

"Detective Bruno Wicks of the Burglary Squad."

"Where'd you meet the man?"

"At school. He wanted me to sign a report about my nights in the park. He had a picture of you in a prison polo shirt."

"Mr. Dalton's disrespectful," the Moose said. "Let me have Robert's knife."

"No knives," the Leader said. "What did this detective say about me, Mr. Dalton?"

"That you'd just got out of Sing Sing."

"It's a bald lie. How could I have whittled that fox? And played chess with your father? Robert, Moosey, how long have I been inhabiting these hills?"

"Years, Leader. Years and years."

"And what's my name, my only name?"

"The Leader."

"That settles it. The case is closed. Harvey Winters White is a detective's dream."

The Leader stooped and picked me up off the ground. The pores in his skin were like pockmarks.

"I'll hurt your mama, Mr. Dalton. I really will. We'll follow you home from your smelly little garden. I'll show you what a firebug is. I'll burn your mama out of bed. What are your instructions, Mr. Dalton?"

I couldn't keep from crying. "Ten dollars a week."

"Every Sunday you leave the gardens and walk outside the gate. We'll signal to you. Don't worry. And if you run to the police, you'll make yourself an absolute orphan. Clear enough? Now go on back to your Victory Garden."

CHAPTER
·16·

I BOUGHT THREE BOTTLES OF ORANGE SODA. One for Mama, one for me, and one for Mauricette. But the gardens were empty except for Mama, who stood outside the gate. The other War Wives had gone home, with Mauricette and Mr. Fink.

"Where were you, Jack? I was worried. Did you have some adventure on the way to the soda man?"

"No, Mama. The vendors were out of orange soda. I had to run to the candy store on Seventy-second Street."

I couldn't have told her about my trial in the woods. I didn't want Mama to burn in her own bed.

We walked out of the park with our hoe. In my mind I kept seeing Harvey Winters White flicking the head of a kitchen match.

I sat in my room, thinking how the Devil must have gotten inside the Leader. The Devil was Harvey Winters White. I stopped reading *The New York Times*. But I didn't suffer. I could still answer all of Dr. Franklin's questions. I'd memorized half the world in a month. I agreed to tutor Arturo. I had to. I had no other means of making money. But Arturo was a bubblehead. He didn't know geography or history. He couldn't find Bataan or Berlin on a map. He couldn't name Hitler's girlfriend, Eva Braun. He only had Hollywood in his head.

"The Coop is from Montana. He started out as a cartoonist."

"Hollywood is Hollywood," I said. "And the world is the world. I don't want to hear about Gary Cooper."

We were at the mansion, sitting in Arturo's study room, which had a desk, an enormous radio, a dictionary, and a cartoon by Gary Cooper of a tiger on a cliff. Mrs. Fink brought us sandwiches and a basket of fruit and cups of hot chocolate with a ball of whipped cream floating in the middle.

I taught Arturo how to read a map and tell from a certain color how high above the sea was a particular portion of land. I taught him how the air was like an ocean, with currents and all. He wouldn't believe me.

"Can you swim in the air?"

"Sometimes," I said. "If it's lively enough."

"Then Superman and Captain Marvel are really swimming in an ocean of air."

"Exactly," I said.

"And they could drown?"

"If the air is turbulent enough."

"Holy Moly," Arturo said, like Captain Marvel. But we couldn't get much further than that. He'd fall asleep after an hour or two. And I only made five dollars that first week.

I was miserable, knowing I'd have to face the Devil, being five dollars short. I did my gardening on Sunday, watching the sweet peas climb their sticks and the potatoes swell in the ground. I told Mama I had to go to the toilet. I walked outside the gate, and there was Robert behind a lamppost. I followed him to the woods, where the Leader was waiting with the Moose.

He mocked that five dollars I'd earned with all the sweat I had. Because it was no picnic trying to teach a bubblehead.

"It's nothing," the Leader shouted, crumpling my five-dollar bill.

"Leader, it's half of ten," Robert said. "Half is half."

"It's nothing."

He shoved the crumpled bill into my shirt. Robert nearly swooned.

"We have a contract, Mr. Dalton. Signed in blood. Your blood. And your mama's."

"Leader," the Moose said. "Ain't it extravagant? Let's keep the fiver."

"No."

"It'll feed us for two days."

"No. All or nothing at all, that's my motto. I'll give him until Tuesday. Then we strike. I'll burn this boy and I'll burn everything around him . . . Now go back to your garden with your five-dollar bill."

And I did, trembling like a winter leaf.

I heard the air-raid sirens. *Whoop, whoop, whoop.* The sweet-pea vines seemed to shiver from all that noise. We had to leave our little gardens and rush inside the gatekeeper's shack. There was a little crowd of War Wives. They all smiled at Mr. Fink. There was Mauricette and me. There was the gatekeeper, who was also an air-raid warden. He put on his warden's white hat. He closed the shutters. He was like the captain of the shack. He carried a whistle around his neck in case any of the gardeners got lost in the middle of an air-raid drill.

I watched Mauricette. I was miserable. I couldn't earn another five dollars in such a short time.

Mauricette must have taken some pity on me. "Jack," she said, "you look ill."

"Shhh," the warden said. "No one's allowed to talk during a drill."

He was a silly man, because even if there were Jap bombers in the sky, they wouldn't have heard us. And they can't understand English anyway.

I listened to the all-clear. It didn't have that horrible *whoop, whoop, whoop*. It was just a slow sad song.

The drill was over. I didn't have to wait for the warden's instructions. I ran out of the shack.

CHAPTER
·17·

I FOUND MY TREASURE CHEST. IT WAS IN THE same bathroom I'd set on fire, on the second floor of Arturo's father's house. Mr. Fink had put in a new mirror. The wall had been repainted where the fire licked. There was a little box for holding Band-Aids in the medicine cabinet behind the mirror. But this box was stuffed with five-dollar bills. It must have been an emergency fund in case the banks ran out of money or the Germans arrived on Seventy-sixth Street.

I took one of the bills.

I went to the park after tutoring Arturo. The hoboes discovered me right away. I gave the Leader all the money I had.

"Now you're a worthy son," he said.

"I'm not your son."

"It's just a figure of speech, Mr. Dalton."

"I'm glad," I said, and I ran away from the hoboes and their Devil, Harvey Winters White.

I didn't eat Mama's mashed potatoes. I wasn't hungry. And I couldn't sleep. I lay down in bed like a little thief. I'd graduated from the Leader's college. And then I realized whose voice it was that told me to set that fire in the sink. Harvey Winters White. I was carrying the Devil's voice around before I ever met the Leader.

That's life. The Devil comes and goes. And I was the betrayer now. I took money from Mr. Fink for tutoring Arturo, I accepted his scholarship at Dutch Masters Day, and I stole from his Band-Aid box to keep the Devil in business. I was more and more miserable. Because I found out the real reason for all those five-dollar bills. Mrs. Fink was going through a crisis. She had a brother in Paris who was hiding from the Nazis. She couldn't write him a letter or call him on the phone, because the telephone exchange was closed between Paris and New York. That's what happens when countries go to war. If Hitler had to call the White House, he'd have to use a Swiss exchange. But Mr. and Mrs. Roosevelt would never accept the call.

All the friends Mrs. Fink had ever had as a child were still in Paris. She'd gone with them to *collège*, which is like Dutch Masters Lower Division, and to the *lycée*, which is like the Upper Division. Her *lycée* was in a place known as the Latin Quarter. It's on a street called St. Andrew of the Arts, and it was taken over by the Nazis during the war and turned into a tiny prison. And Mrs. Fink has nightmares about her old *lycée*. She imagines all her girlfriends and her brother Hugues trapped in the prison, without much nourishment or clothes. The rooms are filled with snow. The walls are frozen. The toilets leak. And sometimes, after she wakes from her dreams, she wanders around the mansion, worrying that it will be another *lycée*. That's why Mr. Fink put boxes stuffed with five-dollar bills in different rooms. The money calms Mrs. Fink. She doesn't feel destitute.

But there's a Nazi in that house. Me. And Mrs. Fink doesn't know it.

It was hard for me to face her, because I understood her trouble. Arturo told me all about it. That's why she goes to the Victory Gardens at late hours. It relaxes her to garden. And she doesn't think about her old *lycée*. But I thought about it lots of times. I wondered if it had its own Harvey Winters White.

I tutored Arturo. I scrubbed the blackboards. I got my gold stars. I wrote a composition about a little girl in the Nazi streets of Paris. Her name was Penelope. She was nine years old. She grew potatoes in her own secret garden. She had to feed her brothers and her sisters and all her cousins who'd lost their mothers and fathers in the war. Penelope had her own special kind of orphanage. She was father, mother, sister, brother, and friend to a whole brood of children.

When it got very cold, Penelope went to a hotel called Uranus, where the Nazis lived, and pretended she was the daughter of a chambermaid. She would steal one pillow at a time. And she'd put the children to bed right inside the pillowcases. But the Nazis caught her and sent Penelope to the prison at St. Andrew of the Arts, where she died of malnutrition.

I read her story to the class like a sad little song. Harriet Godwin started to sniffle.

"It's a heartbreaker," said Barnaby Rosenstock.

Dr. Franklin wiped his eyes with a handkerchief, dismissed the class, and went with me to the principal's office, where I sang the words again. To Mrs. Caroll, who cried and cried.

"Oh, Jack," she said, hugging me hard. "I'm glad I followed my intuition and didn't let you go. You've written a masterpiece."

I won the Dutch Masters Creative Writing Award, which is only given out on rare occasions. Mr. Fink sponsors the award. He arrived that afternoon. I recited Penelope's story a third time. But I didn't feel comfortable in front of Mr. Fink. He must have sensed that Mrs. Fink herself was the model for Penelope.

He didn't cry, like Dr. Franklin and Mrs. Caroll had done. He handed me fifty dollars, since the award carried a cash prize. The fifty dollars came in crumpled five-dollar bills.

I looked into Mr. Fink's eyes and had to fight the shivers. I could tell, as he handed me the cash, that he knew I'd robbed from the Band-Aid box. He didn't shame me in front of Mrs. Caroll. He never said a word.

CHAPTER
·18·

MY COMPOSITION, "PENELOPE'S GHOST," WAS published in the school paper. Mothers and fathers wrote in saying how Penelope had moved them. They wanted more of Penelope. But I couldn't revive a ghost. She'd perished at St. Andrew of the Arts. And I was as miserable as a boy could be, because I'd taken advantage of all the Finks. I was Jack the hypocrite, stealing money and Mrs. Fink's material.

I was glad of one thing. I wouldn't have to raid the Band-Aid box for a while. I could parcel out that cash prize to Harvey Winters White. But when I let him have ten dollars that first Sunday after the award, he pocketed the bills and grabbed me by the throat.

"I hear you came into an inheritance, Mr. Dalton."

"I did not. Who would ever give me an inheritance?"

"Mr. Fink. You won a prize, didn't you? And it's a considerable sum. Fifty dollars."

"But you'll get it all in five weeks."

"That's too slow. I'm your sponsor, ain't I? I coddled you in this park. I was much more attentive to you than your own dead father . . . I want it all."

He started choking me. "I read your story, Mr. Dalton. I saw it in your school's grubby journal. A subscription always arrives in one of our trash barrels. It's sentimental stuff, about the Nazis and one little girl. Whatever talent you have, Mr. Dalton, you got from the Leader. Ain't that right, lads?"

"Yes," shouted Robert and the Moose.

I could hardly breathe, but I saw a raincoat behind the Leader. It belonged to Detective Bruno Wicks. There were other raincoats. Wicks must have brought the whole Burglary Squad. Robert and the Moose began to moan and cry, but Harvey Winters White hadn't seen the raincoats. He was too interested in collecting all my money.

Wicks socked him on the side of the head with a shiny piece of metal. It was one part of a handcuff. The Leader didn't fall. He closed his eyes.

"I'm getting angry," he growled. "I'm getting mad."

Wicks socked him again. Blood flew from a cut in the Leader's head.

"Oh, I'm burning now."

His eyes began to dance in all directions. He was swimming in a sea of air. He tottered and fell face down into the grass.

"Harvey Winters White," Wicks said, "you're under arrest."

CHAPTER
·19·

I WAS MENTIONED IN *THE NEW YORK TIMES*.

"One of the city's most dangerous men, Harvey Winters White, alias the Leader, alias Jefferson Jones, was apprehended on Sunday in Riverside Park, with the help of Jack Dalton, eleven, a student at Dutch Masters Day School. Counseled by the police, young Dalton was instrumental in breaking White's cover as a tramp and in capturing White's accomplices, Robert Stark, thirty-three, and Albert 'Moose' Hawkins, forty-one."

I couldn't have been more of a hero if I'd gone back to Bataan with General MacArthur. Even the Matlocks shook my hand, and that was unthinkable for upperclassmen.

Mauricette dropped a note in my desk. "I forgive you, Jack."

Arturo showed me the letter he'd written to the Coop, telling him how proud he was to have a famous tutor.

Our grocer, Mr. Fish, kept giving Mama bigger and bigger portions of meat.

"Jack," Mama said, "you didn't have to scare the life out of me. You could have told your own mother that you were working for the police."

Neighbors kept offering Mama advice. "Mrs. Dalton, you ought to sue the city. New York's not supposed to use detectives that are underage."

I kept quiet. Whatever I said would be a lie.

I gardened, like I always did, after the Leader's arrest. I caught Mr. Fink near the water fountain. He was wearing a handkerchief on his head, with four little knots, to guard him from getting a sunstroke.

"I'm sorry," I said. "I had to steal from you and Mrs. Fink. The Leader said he'd kill Mama if I didn't give him ten dollars a week."

"We won't discuss it," Mr. Fink said.

"Do you hate me, sir?"

"I don't hate you, Jack."

"Could you ever forgive me?"

"There's nothing to forgive. You'd be a good film producer. You have your own dramatic flair."

"You're the producer, sir. You called the police. That man Wicks couldn't have found the Leader on his own."

"Well, I had a hint. I knew you wouldn't steal without a reason. All I had to do was follow the money . . . It took me to Harvey Winters White."

"But who told *The New York Times* I was working for the police?"

"I did," he said, with the smallest smile. "Now go on back to your garden."

I hated the Leader, but I couldn't help feeling sorry for him. He was like somebody's lost son. Maybe he also had a father who'd died on Bataan. But I doubt it.

I went to the police station on Seventy-seventh Street. There was a sergeant behind the tallest desk I'd ever seen. The sergeant saluted me. He had notebooks and paperweights and old, soiled shirts, a pair of galoshes, and a bottle of ketchup on top of the desk.

"I'm Jack Dalton," I said.

"Is that Detective Jack? Glad to meet ya. How can I help?"

"I'm looking for Bruno Wicks."

"Well, go upstairs then to the Burglary Squad. Second door on the left. And mind your feet. I wouldn't want you tripping on a drunken policeman."

I walked up the stairs. It was very dark. I knocked on the second door and entered a room that was cluttered with desks. Wicks sat with a bunch of other detectives. They looked like a gang of gunmen, with holsters over their hearts. The gunmen were playing cards.

Wicks looked up at me from his desk. "How are you, Dalton?"

"I'd like to see Harvey Winters White."

"What? He's sitting in the Tombs. He was going to strangle you."

"I'd like to see him anyway. He was once my friend."

"He used you, Dalton. He's a user, Harvey is. I should have broken his head."

"I'd like to see him."

Wicks winked at the other gunmen. "Ah, you're talking detective to detective, man to man."

"I'm a boy," I said. "And a retired hobo."

All the gunmen laughed.

CHAPTER
·20·

IT WAS A SAVAGE PLACE, THE TOMBS, A TALL stone camp that held men who were waiting to go on trial. It didn't have windows as far as I could tell, just tiny holes that looked like broken teeth. It could never have suited a citizen of Riverside Park.

I went into the Tombs with a slightly crippled cop that Wicks had lent to me. The gunmen had called him my babysitter.

We got a pass at the front desk. The pass was made of wood, and I had to wear it around my neck, like a cow. We rode up an elevator. I must have been dizzy. I kept seeing spots.

We arrived at a large room that the crippled cop called a bullpen. It had an iron gate right down the middle. The visitors were on one side. The other side had all the locked-up men.

I sat in a chair on my side of the fence and waited for Harvey

Winters White. I waited and waited and suddenly he appeared. He had a tiny bald spot on his head where Wicks had hit him with the handcuff. He had that same dancing look in his eye, like he wasn't sure where he was. He could have been in some bomb shelter. That's what the Tombs was, a bomb shelter, only the bombs were in the Leader's head. But then his eyes stopped dancing, and he was as good as the Devil.

"Ain't we the hero," he said. "My little undercover cop."

"I'm not a cop."

"Yeah, that's what the *Times* says. And I believe the *Times* over you."

"Would the city put a child on the payroll, Mr. Jefferson Jones?"

"Where'd you get that name?" he growled.

"In *The New York Times*."

"Well, it's a falsification. Harvey Winters White is bad enough."

And he sat down on his side of the gate. "I'm penniless," he said, and started to cry.

"Crocodile tears," I told him. "You're just a jailbird who joined the hoboes in Riverside Park."

"Even if I am, I deserve my share of cigarettes. I'm a human being. And I don't have a dime."

"You never met Adolf Hitler in Berlin, did you?"

"I was in Berlin, Connecticut, and Berlin, New Hampshire, and Berlin, Idaho, but not Hitler's Berlin."

"And you weren't a cowboy either."

"Nope. I hate cows."

"You're a fraud, through and through."

"No worse than any man, Mr. Dalton, and better than some."

He wasn't the Devil. He was a broken-down burglar who'd sell his own skull for a cigarette.

"Where were you born, Leader?"

"Across the street from Central Park."

"And what's the name you were born with?"

"Jefferson Jones. My father was a milkman. And he wanted me to follow his footsteps. But I wasn't going to get up at three in the morning and worry about a bunch of milk cans. I told you. I hate cows. I hate milk. I ran away from home. I wasn't even your age, Mr. Dalton. A boy could live around the railroad tracks and never get caught. I started riding the rails. Did ya know there's an entire city of rails in Chicago next to the meat-packing plants? It could house half a million hoboes . . . Forgive me, Mr. Dalton, but I killed a man. It was sort of an accident on purpose. I was seventeen. The law started looking for Jefferson Jones. So I put that name to rest. I liked the feel of Harvey Winters White. It's poetic, ain't it?"

"And what happened to Harvey?"

"I was a victim of circumstance. Had to kill another man. It's my misfortune, killing people. I rode the rails. I started acquiring names. I had six social-security numbers and five birth certificates. I went from Winters White to Peter Abrahams to Archibald Madison to Sidney Caulder and back to Jefferson Jones."

"And Sing Sing."

"Let me finish. It was my downfall, Jefferson Jones. Never did have much luck with that name. It smells of milk. I did two years in Joliet. That's where I got my education as a burglar. Because a man can't live in jail without a little burglarizing. I got out and I burgled and burgled. I was Winters White again. And I wouldn't have been caught if I hadn't put that name on an envelope and written a note to my bank. The bank manager was nosy. He'd read my name on a wanted sign at the post office."

"He called the police."

"He did, he did. And that's how I got to Sing Sing. I swore I'd never use a name again. I'd never have another bank account. I burgled a little when I got out and withdrew from the world. I lived in Riverside Park."

"And called yourself the Leader."

"That was clever of me. Because a nickname isn't legal. It has no repercussions."

"What's a repercussion?"

"A backlash," he said. "I thought you're a writer, Mr. Dalton. You ought to know that word."

"I'm only eleven," I said.

"That's a lame excuse. *Only eleven.* Would Ernest Hemingway ever have said that?"

"Who's Hemingway?"

"Ah, a writer of jungle books . . . I need a cigarette real bad."

"Can't you burgle one?"

"Not in this godforsaken house. It's the Tombs, Mr. Dalton. It's not a place where you can live or die."

"Leader," I said, "would you have strangled me to death if I hadn't given you all my money?"

"I might have, Mr. Dalton. I have a terrific thirst for violence."

"I'll get you a cigarette."

I went over to the guard. "Sir," I said, "that man over there, Harvey Winters White, has been sort of a father to me. Would you get him a cigarette? I can pay you a dollar."

"Not so loud," the guard said. He grabbed my dollar and

whispered to the guard on the other side of the fence. That guard gave Harvey a cigarette, lighting it for him and standing near him while he smoked. The Leader trembled with that cigarette in his mouth.

I couldn't seem to say goodbye. It was too sad, watching Harvey Winters White. I left that bull pen, wearing my wooden visitor's pass, and walked out of the Tombs with that slightly crippled cop.

CHAPTER

·21·

"PENELOPE'S GHOST" BEGAN HAVING REPER-
cussions. *The New York Times* picked it up from our school paper
and reprinted it in a column called "A School Boy's Meditations
on the War." And right away Mrs. Caroll counted up my gold
stars and decided I was valedictorian of the Lower Division, which
means I'd have to deliver a speech at our graduation in June. I
think she slighted Harriet Godwin, who had higher marks than
I did but not as many gold stars.

Harriet was hurt. "Oh," she said, "marks don't matter now that
you're the class celebrity."

"Harriet," I said, "we'll go to Mrs. Caroll. She could have
made a mistake."

"Never mind, Mr. Valedictorian."

And I couldn't help it if I started to strut.

Boys and girls asked me to sign their own copies of my column in the *Times*. I'd write on the newsprint: To Adrienne or Rebecca or Barnaby, With all my feelings. Jack Dalton Junior.

Big Hans saw me from his basement. His eyes were dark and red.

"I'm not a Nazi, Mr. Jack."

"I never said you were."

"But the man who captures the little girl and brings her to the prison on St. Andrew Strasse, his name is Captain Hans."

"It's a story, Hans. It's got nothing to do with fact."

"Then why you call him Hans?"

"Because it's the one German name I knew."

But I should have been more careful about Hans. He'd sat in Ellis Island like a prisoner of war.

"Hansy," I said, "I'll change that captain's name in the second edition . . . if the story is reprinted again. I'll call him Karl."

"Yes," big Hans said. "Karl is good."

And he disappeared into the basement.

I went home. I had to consider my graduation speech. It wasn't like a composition. It had to have its own style, because I'd be talking to teachers and parents and every kid in my class. I couldn't find the music.

The telephone rang. I let it ring and ring. I thought it was one of the neighbors wanting to congratulate little Jack for being in *The New York Times* twice in the same month.

I picked up the phone after the twelfth ring.

"Jack Dalton, we had a date. You were supposed to meet me at the Sugar Bowl . . . for ice-cream sodas."

It was Mauricette.

I still had most of my prize money. I could treat her to a month of ice-cream sodas. But I wasn't so fond of the Sugar Bowl. It reminded me of all my lean years when I couldn't even afford red licorice.

"Coco," I said in my best French. "I was working on my graduation speech and I forgot about the ice-cream sodas."

"Jack, that isn't such a hot start. How can we have a reconciliation?"

I didn't want to lose Mauricette one more time. I couldn't bear it if she was someone else's fiancée.

"I'm getting my coat. I'll be down in ten minutes."

I ran to the Sugar Bowl. It was filled with all my classmates.

"Jack," they shouted. "Jack, Jack, Jack."

Adrienne Rogers flirted with me. Mauricette slapped her wrist.

"Mine is mine, Adrienne. And yours is yours."

"If you keep talking in riddles, Mauricette, I'll never understand you."

"And if you make eyes at Jack, you won't have any eyes."

"You're prehistoric," Adrienne said, and sashayed out of the Sugar Bowl.

I couldn't be alone with my fiancée and talk about our future. Barnaby Rosenstock kept crowding behind me.

"Are you going to have lunch with the Mayor, Jack?"

"Not yet."

"Did you get any letters from Harvard or Yale?"

"Harvard wouldn't write an eleven-year-old."

"You're almost twelve."

"It's still like robbing the cradle."

I looked at Mauricette, and Mauricette looked at me. We both knew we wouldn't get much talking done. I ordered our ice-cream sodas. We'll have to find our future in a much quieter place.

CHAPTER
·22·

MAMA HAD TO FIX UP MY ROBERT HALL SUIT OR I'd have nothing to graduate in. The suit was torn from the time I was a hobo in Riverside Park. Mama replaced the buttons that were lost. She patched up the pockets. She made me a fresh pair of cuffs. Sewing parachutes had turned her into a tailor.

I couldn't finish my speech.

I'd imagine the Leader in his cell at the Tombs and my whole body would shiver. He'd marked me, that old man. I couldn't seem to recover from Harvey Winters White.

I scribbled ten pages about what it meant to graduate in the middle of a war. I mentioned MacArthur and Hitler and the Home Front. I mentioned ration stamps and meatless nights. I mentioned false coffee and fake ham. It was as patriotic a speech as I could ever write.

I took it with me to graduation. Mama was sitting in the front row of the auditorium with Mr. and Mrs. Fink, who had a glaze in her eye. I could tell. Part of her was in Paris. She'd lost her *lycée* and her childhood friends, so it must have upset her to see other children, even her own child, in an American *collège*.

I was up on the stage with Arturo and the rest of the class. Arturo looked miserable. Mr. Fink had sponsored me, not him. I'd stolen some of his father, some of his "old man."

Mrs. Caroll was with us. She was proud as hell. It was the best sort of graduation for her. Because she couldn't lose us. We'd get rid of our graduation gowns, have the summer to ourselves, and come right back to her at the Upper Division.

But she had to cry a little.

"Graduates, parents, and friends," she said, installing herself behind the speaker's stand. "I must disappoint you. Mr. Burton Fink, president of our board of trustees, had arranged to have a secret guest. Gary Cooper."

The whole auditorium sighed.

"But, alas, he could not come. He has a murderous shooting schedule in Hollywood. But he did send us a telegram. And I'll read it to you. 'Dear Mrs. Caroll, Please give my apologies to the class of 1943. I was hoping to share this day with them in person, but we had to reshoot some scenes from Mr. Hemingway's *For Whom the Bell Tolls*. I'm honored to be in a film that tells about our fight against Fascism. And I know that all of you at Dutch Masters are fighting that fight. With my deepest respect, Gary Cooper.' "

We clapped. The girls cried. But I was a little suspicious. The Leader had said that Mr. Hemingway wrote jungle books. *For Whom the Bell Tolls* didn't feel like any film about a jungle book. I'd have to ask the school librarian.

Mrs. Caroll kept talking for a couple of minutes and then she introduced me. "This year's valedictorian is an unusual one. He's already a published author. He's the revelation of his own class. A boy who was on the brink of suspension, who'd become a truant. And made a startling recovery. Jack Dalton Junior."

I took Mrs. Caroll's place at the speaker's stand. There was more clapping for me than for Gary Cooper's telegram. I put my speech on top of the stand. I looked out at the auditorium. It was like a sea of faces. And I was getting sick. I didn't feel like talking about Hitler and fake ham. I closed one eye and let the words fall from my mouth.

"I met a hobo in Riverside Park. He's more of a burglar than a patriot. Harvey Winters White." And I talked about the son of a milkman who went on the road, a road of tracks. "He couldn't even keep his own name."

The auditorium was fidgeting at first. I didn't care. I had a story to tell. But people began to warm to Harvey Winters White. "He's a murderer," I said. "I don't deny it. But he's also a boy who made so many false moves he couldn't really start his life."

There were handkerchiefs among that sea of faces, handkerchiefs among the women and men.

"He tried to steal my dowry, the prize I got from Mr. Fink. But I wouldn't be here, as your valedictorian, if it hadn't been for Harvey Winters White. He taught me how to read *The New York Times* and how to tell a story, to invent things along a crooked line.

"Harvey's sitting in the Tombs," I said. "And I'm the valedictorian of my class. It's too late for Harvey. But if he'd had a hobo at the right minute, a hobo to teach him more than tricks, to smash the head of a pumpkin and discover the flesh inside, he might have become his own kind of valedictorian."

I went back to my seat on stage. Mrs. Caroll kissed me. "Another masterpiece."

Arturo was blubbering. "I need Harvey," he said.

Mauricette passed me a note. *You can invite that murderer to our wedding.*

I went home with Mama.

We ate out at the Automat. I could never figure how the girl in the change booth could feed you twenty nickels so quick. She didn't count them one at a time. She had a musical fist that could feel bunches of nickels in fives or tens, twenties or thirties even.

I kept going to the little glass windows and putting nickels into the slot. The windows would open and let you have a pineapple salad.

I always had a feast at the Automat.

When we returned, the telephone was ringing.

I picked up the phone.

"Coco," I said, "how are you?"